Access for Beginners
ACCESS ESSENTIALS BOOK 1

M.L. HUMPHREY

SELECT TITLES BY M.L. HUMPHREY

ACCESS ESSENTIALS
Access for Beginners
Intermediate Access

EXCEL ESSENTIALS
Excel for Beginners
Intermediate Excel
50 Useful Excel Functions
50 More Excel Functions

WORD ESSENTIALS
Word for Beginners
Intermediate Word

POWERPOINT ESSENTIALS
PowerPoint for Beginners
Intermediate PowerPoint

BUDGETING FOR BEGINNERS
Budgeting for Beginners
Excel for Budgeting

CONTENTS

INTRODUCTION

Microsoft Excel is my first love. And my go-to program for when I need to do a calculation or track data. But the fact of the matter is, there are times when Excel just doesn't cut it. Most notably, when I'm trying to combine information from more than one source and generate summaries of that information. That's where Microsoft Access comes into play.

(Now, technically, I think Excel in recent versions has been amended so that you could potentially combine multiple data sources within Excel much like you can do in Access, but I tried playing with it once, found it horrifying, and quickly retreated back to using Access. So we'll ignore that possibility for now.)

I've also used Access over Excel in the past when I had large amounts of text that I needed to store and make available to users. (I've created some massive text-based spreadsheets in Excel in the past, but at a certain point the text just doesn't display well. You have to manually resize each row to make all the text visible and sometimes even that doesn't work.)

So those are my two default reasons for using Access: when I need to link data across multiple sources to create summary reports or analysis and when the data I need to track includes very lengthy text fields.

This is because I come to Access as someone used to using Excel rather than as a database expert.

It's important to understand this because it will impact the way in which I teach Access and the strengths and weaknesses I personally see in using Access. If you're a database person, this may not be the book for you. But if you're familiar with Excel and looking for additional capabilities that Excel can't give you, then this book could be the perfect place to start.

I should also add here that as I write this in late 2019 I think Access fills a unique but shrinking role. When it was first released I would bet that there weren't a lot of off-the-shelf options available for building your own point of sale database or tracking customer contact information, and that Access was a good tool for filling that need.

But anymore I think there are a number of commercially-available solutions that do a better job and probably come with far less potential for error. So if you're a small business and looking to create a customer contact database or track your accounting information, I'd check the available off-the-shelf solutions first before I tried to create a custom Access database.

And if you're at a larger company, talk to your IT department before you use Access. You might be surprised what they already have available.

For example, many years ago I had to send out a questionnaire to five hundred brokerage firms about their business activities. That's something that if left to my own devices I might've done via a paper questionnaire and then tracked through Access. But it turned out my company had a very simple but effective software program that allowed them to build an online questionnaire to my specifications and export the results to an Excel spreadsheet.

So I know those types of solutions are out there and I would argue that they're probably easier to use than Access and less prone to data integrity issues.

Also, if you find yourself dealing with significant amounts of data then Access may not be advanced enough for what you need and you should explore more sophisticated options.

For example, I know just enough about the R programming language to know that I could probably write a script that would do in R what I currently do in Access for my sales tracking. And that if I were to do so it would require less time and effort each month for me to generate my reports. But right now the amount of data I'm working with doesn't require something that sophisticated. If I were dealing with millions of records each month, it might make sense to explore a better solution than Access.

At this point you may be wondering what I think Access actually is good for.

Where I see Access still having tremendous value is in taking custom data sets from different sources, combining that data, and then generating summary reports on that data.

For example, I sell my books through eleven different distributors. Access is perfect for combining the sales information across those eleven distributors into simple reports that let me see revenue, expenses, and profits by title, series, author, and genre.

There are pre-packaged commercial solutions out there for authors who use only one platform (Amazon) and other solutions for authors who use a handful of the largest distributors, but there are none that allow the level of customization I need.

Also, because the distributors I sell through don't always tell anyone before making changes to their reports, the available commercial solutions sometimes break unexpectedly. Not their fault—those changes break my Access database too—but that means it's possible for a user to not have access to reporting until those products are updated. (Or worse, they might miss a change and not even know it.) By creating a custom Access database that I control, I can fix my reports immediately and I know when something is off.

Also, with a custom database I can add new reports as needed. I'm not at the mercy of someone else's development schedule or choices.

Access is the perfect solution for creating that kind of database. And I expect it will continue to be so into the future.

So that's where I'm coming from in this book. And that's how I'll approach teaching you Access.

My goal in this book is to educate you enough so that you're able to upload either Excel or .csv files into your database, link them to one another, and then create select queries that combine information pulled from more than one data table or query at a time. And I'll be doing so with the perspective of an Excel user.

To make that happen we'll first discuss how Access databases work, the four main components of Access, the key differences I see between working in Access and Excel, and then how to complete basic tasks in Access as well as navigate through the various parts of Access.

Once we have that foundation established, we'll discuss the two ways to create tables, how to export an existing Access data table or query to Excel, how to add data to a table from an external Excel file, the most common field data types, table views, and how to amend data in a table.

We'll then discuss how to perform various tasks in tables and queries, such as selecting records or columns and changing row heights or column widths.

From there we'll cover select queries including how to create a basic detail query and how to create a basic summary query using only one table or query as the source. This will be done using the Query Wizard. We'll also cover the types of query views available and the Design View in particular.

Next we'll discuss table relationships and how to use them to create detail and summary queries that use more than one table or query as their source. And we'll discuss how to use basic criteria to narrow down the results in a query.

Finally we'll cover summary results, sorting data, and filtering data in tables and queries. And then we'll finish with a brief discussion about forms, reports, and printing.

By the time you're done with this book you should be able to comfortably navigate Access and work with tables and queries at a beginner level.

I want to give you enough information to get started in Access without overwhelming you, which means topics like how to customize forms and reports and how to create union or crosstab queries aren't covered here. Those topics along with others are covered in detail in *Intermediate Access*, the next book in this series.

If you are already familiar with another Microsoft Office product, like Excel, the beginning of this book may seem too simplistic to you because I am going to start at the beginning as if you know nothing about opening an Access database. But Access does differ from the other Office products in certain respects, so I'd still recommend skimming those sections.

Also, this book is written using Access 2013. That means all of the screenshots from the book and all of the navigation instructions are based on the 2013 version of Access. What I'm going to cover here should be mostly the same for all versions of Access from Access 2007 onward, but just be aware of that fact in case something doesn't look or work the same.

Alrighty then. Let's start with some basic terminology.

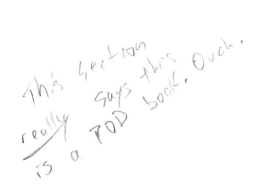

This section really says this is a POD book. Ouch.

BASIC TERMINOLOGY

Before we get started, I want to make sure that we're on the same page in terms of terminology. Some of this will be standard to anyone talking about Access and some of it is my personal quirky way of saying things, so best to skim through if nothing else.

Tab

I refer to the menu choices at the top of the screen (File, Home, Create, External Data, Database Tools, etc.) as tabs. If you click on one you'll see that the way it's highlighted sort of looks like an old-time filing system.

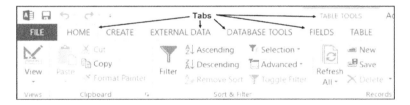

Each tab you select will show you different options. For example, in the image above, I have the Home tab selected and you can do various tasks such as change views, cut/copy/paste, sort and filter, refresh your data, add/save/delete a record, add a totals row, check spelling, and more. Other tabs give other options.

Click

If I tell you to click on something, that means to use your mouse (or trackpad) to move the cursor over to a specific location and left-click or right-click on the option. (See the next definition for the difference between left-click and right-click).

If you left-click, this selects the item. If you right-click, this generally creates a dropdown list of options to choose from. If I don't tell you which to do, left- or right-click, then left-click.

5

Left-click/Right-click

If you look at your mouse or your trackpad, you generally have two flat buttons to press. One is on the left side, one is on the right. If I say left-click that means to press down on the button on the left. If I say right-click that means press down on the button on the right.

Not all trackpads have the left- and right-hand buttons. In that case, you'll basically want to press on either the bottom left-hand side of the trackpad or the bottom right-hand side of the trackpad.

Dropdown Menu

If you right-click on something, for example a field or table name, in Access you will see what I'm going to refer to as a dropdown menu. (Sometimes it will actually drop upward if you're towards the bottom of the screen.)

A dropdown menu provides you a list of choices to select from like this one that you'll see if you right-click on a field in a new table:

There are also dropdown menus available for some of the options listed under the tabs at the top of the screen. For example, if you go to the Home tab, you'll see small arrows below or next to some of the options, like the View option and the Refresh All option on the Home tab. Clicking on those little arrows will give you a dropdown menu with a list of choices to choose from.

Expansion Arrows

I don't know the official word for these, but you'll also notice at the bottom right corner of most of the sections in each tab that there are little arrows. If you click on one of those arrows Access will bring up a more detailed set of options, usually through a dialogue box (which we'll discuss next) or by adding another pane (which we'll define after that).

In the Home tab, for example, there are expansion arrows for Clipboard and Text Formatting. Holding your mouse over the arrow will give a brief description of what clicking on the expansion arrow will do like here for the Clipboard section on the Home tab:

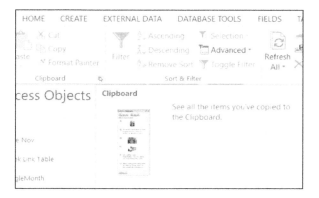

Dialogue Box

Dialogue boxes are pop-up boxes that cover specialized settings. As just mentioned, if you click on an expansion arrow, it will often open a dialogue box that contains more choices than are visible in that section. When you click on the expansion arrow for the Text Formatting section of the Home tab, for example, that brings up the Datasheet Formatting dialogue box which looks like this:

While Access does have some dialogue boxes, they aren't near as common as in Excel. But you will see them for certain tasks like, for example, printing.

Panes

When you first open an Access database you will notice that there is a main workspace on the right-hand side, which opens with a new table, Table1. This takes up most of the screen.

On the left-hand side of that table, however, is what I'm going to refer to as a pane. In this case it's the All Access Objects pane. You can see the title at the top and it takes up about one-fifth of the left-hand side of the view area.

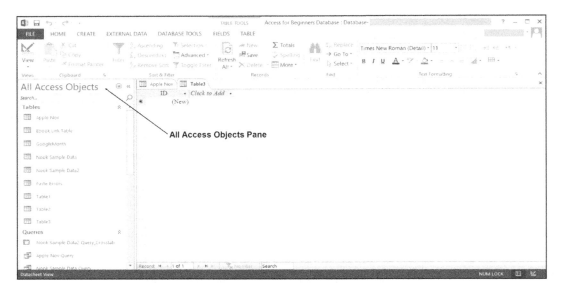

A pane is a separate section that contains information or options aside from what you see in the main workspace. (Panes often show up in PowerPoint as well.)

The All Access Objects pane is where you go to easily navigate between your tables, queries, forms, and reports. It can be minimized but not closed.

Other panes can be opened and closed as needed and will appear on either the left-hand side or the right-hand side of the main workspace depending on the pane.

To see an example of one that can be closed, click on the expansion arrow in the Clipboard section of the Home tab to open the Clipboard pane. It should open on the left side of the All Access Objects pane. Below I've zoomed in the view so you can see it clearly.

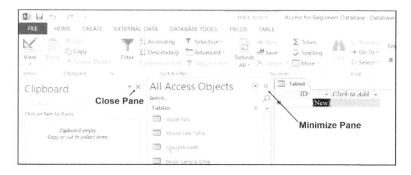

To close a pane, click on the X in the top right corner of the pane.

If instead of an X there is a double-arrow in the top right corner (like with the All Access Objects pane as you can see above) you can click on the double arrow to either minimize the pane or expand it. (Note that when what I refer to as the All Access Objects pane is minimized Access refers to it as the Navigation Pane. The name displays in the middle of the minimized space)

To change the width of a pane, hold your mouse over the inner edge of the pane until you see a double-sided arrow pointing left and right, left-click, and drag until the pane is your desired width.

Scroll Bar

Scroll bars allow you to see your data when there is sufficient data to take up more space than is currently available on the screen.

When you have enough tables, queries, reports, and forms, there will be a scroll bar visible on the right-hand side of the All Access Objects pane.

Also, when the data in your table, query, form, or report has more content than will fit on the screen, there will be scroll bars visible in the main workspace.

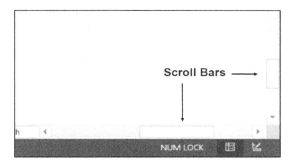

In the image above there are scroll bars on both the right-hand side and the bottom. The mouse (which is shown as an arrow) is pointing at the right-hand scroll bar and you can see that there is gray space on either side of the scroll bar as well as arrows at the end of the gray space.

To move through your data using the scroll bar, you can either left-click on the bar itself, hold the left-click, and drag the bar along the gray area. Or you can click in the gray area to either side of the scroll bar to move in that direction a smaller amount. Or you can click on the arrows visible at the ends of the gray space.

Clicking on the gray space moves you one screen at a time. Clicking on the arrow at the end moves you one row or column at a time. Clicking and dragging the scroll bar will move you multiple rows or columns at a time; how fast that happens depends on how fast you drag the scroll bar.

Arrow

If I ever tell you to arrow to the left or right or up or down, that just means use your arrow keys. If you're clicked onto a cell (which we'll define shortly) this usually will move you to the left one cell, to the right one cell, up one cell, or down one cell. However, if you are double-clicked into a cell so that you can edit the text, arrowing right or left will move you to the right or left one character space within the cell.

Tab Through or Tab To

I may instead tell you to tab through or tab to your data. This is different from the tabs we discussed above. In this instance, we're talking about using the Tab key. If you are in a cell and you use the Tab key it will move you to the right one cell. If it's the end of the row it will move you to the first cell of the next row.

Using the Shift key and the Tab key together will move you to the left one cell. If you're at the beginning of a row it will move you to the end of the row just above.

(Using the Tab key is a handy way to highlight an entire cell if you need to copy the value for some reason. Click on a cell to either side, Tab or Shift + Tab to get into the cell you want, and then copy using Ctrl + C.)

Cursor

There are two possible meanings for cursor. When you're clicked into a cell in a data table, you will see that there is a blinking line. This indicates where you are in the cell. If you type text, each letter will appear where the cursor was at the time you typed it. The cursor will move (at least in the U.S. and I'd assume most European versions) to the right as you type. This version of the cursor should be visible at all times when you're working in a data table.

The other type of cursor is the one that's tied to the movement of your mouse or trackpad. When you're typing, it will not be visible. But stop typing and move your mouse or trackpad, and you'll see it.

If this cursor is positioned over your data, it will usually look somewhat like a tall skinny capital I. If you move it up to the menu options or off to the sides, it becomes a white arrow. (Except for when you position it over any option under the tabs that can be typed in such as font size or font where it will once again look like a skinny capital I.)

It can also look like a small squat cross or a double-sided arrow at times depending on what you're able to do at that moment.

Usually I won't refer to your cursor, I'll just say, "click" or "select" or whatever action you need to take with it. Moving the cursor to that location will be implied.

Table

There are actually two different types of tables I talk about in Access.

Later when we discuss the four main components of an Access database, one of those will be Tables. In that meaning, tables are data tables where your imported or input data is stored.

But if you look at a query in Datasheet View, this too is what I would describe as a table of data because the information is stored in columns and rows like you would see in an Excel worksheet.

Column/Field

Every table in Access consists of rows and columns of information. Columns, which can also be referred to as fields, run across the top of the workspace and are named Field1, Field2, etc. by default. The name of each column/field can be changed to a user-provided name.

In the image below, the columns/fields in this table are ID, Month, Year, and Field1.

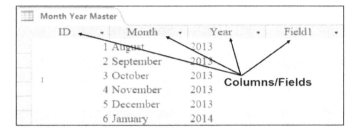

Row/Record

Rows/records run downward in a data table.

The table pictured above has six rows/records in it. In that case there is an ID field and those records are numbered sequentially. But they don't have to be.

In the below image we have a table with four records in it. Note that the record with an ID of 1 has been deleted so there is no longer a record with an ID of 1 in the table and that the other records are not in sequential order anymore because the table is sorted on the values in Field1 rather than on ID.

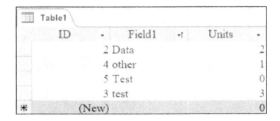

That ID column is optional. It does not have to be a part of your table.

If there is an ID number in a table that ID number will be tied to the record in that particular row so that if you change the sort order of your data the ID number moves with its record. This is different from how Excel works where the row number is tied to the row and exists for ease of reference.

So while a data table in Access can look much like a worksheet in Excel, it works very differently. Think of each row of a data table in Access as containing a related set of information that will always stay together. Technically, this is best referred to as a record. However, because I approach Access as an Excel user I may still sometimes refer to rows of data.

Cell or Entry or Value

When I refer to a cell in Access I am referring to the intersection of a column and row. So, in the Columns screenshot above the Year associated with the record with ID 4 is 2013. That value, 2013, is stored in a cell.

Cell is once more terminology that I bring over from using Excel.

It is probably more appropriate to refer to values or entries but in a generic sense I will still say something like, "click into the cell next to the cell that contains the value you want to copy."

Control Shortcuts

In Access there are various control shortcuts that you can use to perform tasks like save, copy, cut, and paste. I don't use control shortcuts near as much in Access as I do in Excel or Word, but they are available.

Each time I refer to one it will be written as Ctrl + a capital letter, but when you use the shortcut on your computer you don't need to use the capitalized version of the letter.

For example, holding down the Ctrl key and the c key at the same time will copy any highlighted entry. I'll write this as Ctrl + C, but that just means hold down the key that says Ctrl and the c key at the same time.

Undo

Access does have an Undo option which will generally let you undo your last action. It's available in the Quick Access Toolbar in the top left corner of the screen or by using Ctrl + Z.

However, Undo is not nearly as powerful in Access as it is in Excel or in Word and you should not rely on it. You can only undo one single action in Access. If you deleted 500 rows, it will bring one back. And sometimes it doesn't work at all. Or it undoes one type of action while you were hoping it would undo another.

So be very careful with your entries and be sure to save a copy of your database before you start doing anything that might break it or change large amounts of your data, because in Access you will not be able to get that information back or reverse those changes the way you would be able to in Excel.

HOW AN ACCESS DATABASE WORKS

Alright, now that we've covered basic terminology we need to take a crash course in how databases work and why you use them.

At its most basic, a database stores information and organizes that information for easy search and retrieval. Technically an Excel worksheet is a database. It's called a flat file database. Everything is stored in one set of rows and columns in a single table.

What Access lets you do is create what's called a relational database where you can take multiple tables of data and relate them to one another to create more complex reports. Access is what's referred to as a database management system (DBMS).

There are two main reasons, in my opinion, to work with relational databases.

One, it allows you to keep from repeating the same information over and over and over again. This saves potential data entry errors as well as takes up less space, which can be important when dealing with a large set of data.

So rather than have customer first name, customer last name, street address, city, state, and zip code followed by transaction amount and transaction date for every single transaction a company does, you can store in one location one time the customer information and then link that to a unique Customer ID. You can then create another table where you list Customer ID, transaction date, and transaction amount.

Because you have the Customer ID in both locations any time you want to you can pull in that customer information without having to repeat it and store it for every single customer transaction. This can be a significant savings in terms of space used and computation time.

Why? Let's look at this in more detail.

There are six pieces of information we've collected on this customer (first name, last name, street address, city, state, and zip code). For every transaction we also collect transaction date and amount. That's eight pieces of information per transaction.

If we had five transactions for Customer Jones that's forty pieces of information we'd need to store using a flat file database.

However, in a relational database, like Access, you can take the six pieces of customer information and turn them into one Customer ID. Now we have three pieces of information per transaction (Customer ID, transaction date, and transaction amount) plus the six pieces of customer data and their identifier.

That means we only have to store twenty-two pieces of information (three times five plus seven). That's just a little over half as much information as before.

Right there, for one customer with five transactions, you've almost halved your data storage requirements. Multiply that times thousands of customers and thousands of transactions and you can begin to see how powerful using a relational database can be, especially if you're trying to perform calculations on that data.

(Although as discussed in the introduction, when you reach the point where this really starts to matter, I think Access is no longer the best solution.)

The second use for a relational database, and why I use Access the most, is that it allows you to take data from multiple sources and tie them together to create summaries of that information.

So, for example, let's say I have sales reports from three different vendors for twenty different books. Each of those vendors gives me sales reports with different columns of information and with different identification numbers for each book.

Vendor A labels my first book AEFG345. Vendor B labels it 123578. Vendor C labels it H2T45.

Ideally they would all use the same title that I gave them, but they don't. Sometimes they add the subtitle. One vendor adds the library name to the title every single time a book sells to a library so that in their reports one single title can be referred to by an infinite number of names.

This means I can't just copy and paste the title, units sold, and amount earned from those three vendor reports into an Excel worksheet and create a pivot table to see total sales.

Because I have nothing to effectively link the data across those reports. The identifiers are different and the titles are different.

But what I can do is put those three vendor reports into Access, add one more table where I tell Access that for Title A the identifier is AEFG345 at Vendor A, 123578 at Vendor B, and H2T45 at Vendor C. I can then build a query to pull the sales information for that title from all three reports.

The key with a relational database is that the different tables of data need to link to one another somehow. They need to have a relationship.

To create a relational database you need to tell Access how the data in Table 1 relates to the data in Table 2. Your whole relational database is based on, no surprise here, relationships between your different data tables.

In the customer transaction example I walked through above, we had Customer ID to link the customer information table to the customer transaction table. That is the traditional way of working with a relational database.

You have a customer information table with Customer ID. You have a product table with Product ID. You have a branch office table with Branch ID. You have a Sales Representative or Employee table with Sales Representative ID or Employee ID. And then you have a table with more granular transaction information that leverages those IDs.

So you might list transaction date, Customer ID, Product ID, Sales Rep ID, and sales amount for a transaction. Transaction date and sales amount are unique to that transaction. The rest can be referred to using the ID numbers.

Basically, you're taking one big set of data and extracting the bits that repeat themselves and replacing them with an identifier.

That is the traditional way that people use relational databases.

The way I use a relational database is a bit backwards from that.

As I mentioned above, I take unrelated reports—the reports from each of my vendors—and build a master table that tells Access how to relate them to one another. Think of the master table I use as a decoder key. It says that for Product A when we're looking at Table 1, this is how it's identified. When we're looking at Table 2, this is how it's identified. And in Table 3, this is how it's identified.

Using a master table like that lets me go to each separate vendor and pull in the information for that product no matter how that vendor has chosen to identify that product or what order they've chosen to provide their information in.

But even though my approach is vastly different than the standard approach, at heart both approaches are still based on relationships.

For either approach to work, you must have unique identifiers in each table that you can link to.

You can't have 123 be the Customer ID for both Customer Jones and Customer Smith in the same data table. 123 must be the Customer ID for one unique customer in that data table and that cannot change or be reused.

Also, when you're building your database, you have to make sure that there is something in each table of data that can be linked to your other tables of data, and that the value you choose to link on is unique to that product, customer, etc. within that data table.

We'll walk through this more later, so if it sounds confusing right now, don't worry.

The basic message to take away here is that Access works by taking different tables of data and linking them to one another so that you can then create queries that pull that information together into one central location when needed.

This section still does not fill me w/ confidence.

demographics —— *offense*
—— *commitments*
—— *sentences*
—— *assessments*

On Average, how many Assessments/person?

FOUR MAIN COMPONENTS OF AN ACCESS DATABASE

Okay. So now that you have the basic idea of what we're trying to do by using Access: upload various tables of information and then link them so we can create queries based on what's in more than one of those tables, let's walk through the four main components of an Access database.

(As determined by me based on the way Access is organized.) ← *Terrifying*

Those components are Tables, Queries, Forms, and Reports.

Each one that you create within your Access database will be shown by default in its own section in your All Access Objects pane. Like so:

Tables

Tables are the bedrock upon which everything else is built. As a matter of fact, everything else would be blank without your data tables because all the other three components do is store a way to pull or display the data that's kept in your tables. Each time you generate a query, report, or form, it pulls the information it uses from your tables.

Delete your tables and your queries, forms, and reports will be blank.

That's why tables are listed at the top. This is your raw data. This is primarily where you input, edit, and delete the information used in your database.

Each table should be unique in terms of what it contains. You shouldn't need to have multiple tables with the same information in them.

In my database, for example, I have a tables of sales information for each vendor as well as my master title table that links it all together.

In a more traditional database there might be customer data, product data, employee data, transaction data, and sales tax data tables.

It is up to the user(s) of the Access database to define what columns of data are in each table and provide the values that go into each record.

You can create tables manually, directly in Access, and also input information directly into a table in Access. Or you can do what I do for the most part which is upload data to Access to either create a table or add new records to that table.

(Don't worry, we'll walk through how to do both options later. The key right now is that tables are what everything else depends on and where your data is stored.)

Queries

Queries are where you tell Access how to pull together the information in your various data tables or from other queries.

If you think of your data tables as a big juicy buffet of food, then a query is the equivalent of going through that buffet and loading up a plate with just the items you want. You take a little bit of customer information from here, a little bit of product information from there, add in some cost data and sales data, and now you have a query that shows you profit and loss by product and customer.

Queries are where the bulk of the analysis is done. Your tables are the raw material, your queries are where you put that material together to make something useful.

I have far more queries than tables. When I was preparing to write this book I counted and I had twenty-two tables of data and one hundred and ten queries.

(Before you panic, understand that those queries grew organically over time as I decided I needed more information. And that some are a simple copy and paste of others. For example, I have a series of queries that pull data for 2018. When 2019 rolled around I simply copied those queries and changed the year criteria from 2018 to 2019. Voila. Five new queries in less than ten minutes.)

So queries are where you pick and choose the information you want and combine it together in a way that works for you.

Forms

Forms are something I have used for corporate clients in the past, but that I don't tend to use for my own Access database. A form displays each record from a table in a more user-friendly way. It's like someone took all that data you input and printed it on a letter-size piece of paper with nice formatting.

You can have Access take a data table and create a form for you. This is an example of what a form that Access created from a table that had three fields (ID, Field1, Field 2) looks like:

For some users, this is much more manageable than the standard columns and rows set-up of a table.

Now, the interesting thing about a form is that you can actually make edits to the values on the form and those will change the values in your table as well. (Except the identifier field which is set up to be a non-changeable value that identifies the record.)

If you are going to input your data directly into Access, as opposed to upload it like I normally do, then having a form can make the process more user-friendly. Instead of trying to tab through little boxes in a grid of rows and columns, you can work with text boxes that look like a form you'd fill out at the DMV.

Forms are especially useful when you're dealing with entries that contain a large amount of text.

But the thing to be careful of is that an edit to a value in a form is also an edit to your underlying data table, and those changes are saved the minute they're made. And, as I've mentioned more than once at this point, there are probably better commercially-available options out there if you need to collect information directly like you would through a form that don't expose you to the same risk of data loss.

Also, not here that the default format for a form is one record per page, but forms can be set up to display multiple records at once.

Reports

Reports are just what they sound like, reports. They take the information you have in a table or query and they put it in a report format that has better formatting for print or distribution.

In a report you can change the font or font size, add section headers and footers, add subtotals by section, only include certain fields, arrange how the fields appear on the page, and more.

A report can pull from multiple sources, but I tend to use methods for generating reports that require that all of the information be in a single query or table already.

* * *

As I mentioned previously, this book focuses on creating tables and basic queries. At the very end we will cover how to generate a basic report or form, but customizing either one is beyond the scope of this book. I just wanted you to know what the four components of Access are so that you're familiar with them if you see them.

Okay. Now let's discuss the key differences between Access and Excel that make working in Access far more dangerous than working in Excel.

ACCESS VERSUS EXCEL AND THE DANGERS OF WORKING IN A DATABASE ENVIRONMENT

One of my favorite things to say when talking about Excel is that Ctrl + Z, Undo, is your friend. In Excel if you write a formula wrong or delete the wrong data or sort wrong or filter wrong, you just Ctrl + Z or click on the little Undo button on the ribbon until you're back to where you were before.

That is not the case with Access.

Let me repeat but in a slightly different way.

Access *does* have an Undo option, but it is extremely limited. It will undo exactly one thing and one thing only. So if you edit one thousand records at once, it will undo one of those edits and only one of those edits. Also, it doesn't undo everything. Sometimes you do something in Access, realize you made a mistake, and there's no going back.

That's because Access is at heart a database application. It is meant to store data and then to allow you to use that data for reports and calculations. The nature of a database like that is that you change a record and the change sticks. There is no, "Well, I didn't save so I can just close it and we'll be fine" with Access.

Oh no.

The minute you delete a value and move on to a new record, that value is gone. You can't get it back. If you overwrite a value and move on, that value is overwritten. If you put in a garbage entry in Access, that value is saved. As soon as you make a change to a record in a table and move on, that change sticks. This includes if you make a change to that table through a simple query or through a form.

(For formatting or design changes, Access will ask if you want to save them. But not data changes.)

This is why I prefer to make any adjustments to my raw data outside of Access. (It's also why I keep my raw data files forever so that if I mess up with my adjustments I can always go back to the raw data and start over. Just delete the bad data in Access and upload the revised data.)

That's why I also am not a fan of direct data entry in Access, because there's no backup if you get it wrong.

The other reason I prefer to work in Excel first is because Access views every single record in a data table as its own standalone record.

What that means practically speaking is that you can't copy and paste a value down an entire column easily the way you can in Excel. So, for example, if I want to enter "Mystery" in a hundred rows in Excel I can type it once, copy it, and paste it down the next 99 rows. I'm done in ten seconds. In Access, it doesn't work that way. You'd have to paste it into each of those 99 records and it would probably take five minutes.

In Excel I can also go to the next row, start to type "m" and as long as there are no other entries that start with an m, Excel will suggest "mystery" for my value. Again, that doesn't happen in Access because each record is treated separately.

So while the data tables in Access and Excel look a lot alike, they do not in fact behave a lot alike.

You may be thinking to yourself, when would this even come into play?

Well, let me give you an example. I get vendor reports that I upload to Access on a monthly basis. And I like to know my sales by month for each product. But most of the vendor reports I receive only use a date. Or, worse, they use a date range which sometimes crosses months. It's not very easy then to pull out the month of the transaction using a formula.

But since I know what month that report pertains to when I upload it, I add two additional columns—month and year—to my Excel spreadsheet before I upload it. This lets me easily pull a report of sales by month/year for every product on every vendor.

I can add those two columns to my data in Excel in less than a minute. I add the values to the two columns in the first row, highlight those entries, double-click in the bottom right corner to copy to the rest of the rows, change the setting so that it's a copy of those values and not a series, and I'm done.

In Access? Well, just image I have a thousand records where I have to add a month and year and I can't set up a rule because next month it'll be a different month and maybe a different year. I'd have to go through and add my month first to all thousand records. Then I'd have to do the same for year. I can't do them together.

Access is built for data entry of one record at a time where that record is treated as separate and standalone. Excel is not. So by working in Excel I can save substantial amounts of time.

If this doesn't make sense to you now, don't worry. Either you're not so ingrained in working with Excel that it'll be an issue for you or you'll start to understand what I'm talking about as you work in Access. The main caution here is to be careful when working in your data tables that you don't accidentally delete any information or edit information you didn't want to edit. And to think when entering data whether you could do so more effectively in Excel instead of Access.

Also, the fact that it's so easy to permanently alter a record in Access is why people will advise you to backup your Access database frequently. That way at least if you make some horrible, irreparable mistake you can just go back to the prior version.

(I will confess I don't do this. When I'm about to make a major change to my database I will back it up so that if my change fails I can ditch the new version, but because I keep my raw data elsewhere I know I can always rebuild my entire database in a relatively short period of time. And maybe even improve on it while I'm at it. Don't be like me, though. It's poor practice to work that way.)

If you're using your Access database for original data entry definitely back that puppy up. Daily. You have nowhere else to get that information, so don't risk losing it or overwriting it.

And, seriously, consider what you're doing given your available options in the market today. Is using an Access database in that way really the best idea for your business?

Okay. Off my high horse. Next let's quickly cover the basics of working in Access, starting with how to create a new database, save it, delete, and rename it.

ABSOLUTE BASICS

If you've read any of the introductory books I've written on Excel, Word, or PowerPoint, you already know most of this. Although there are a few key differences when dealing with Access that might be worth knowing. For those who haven't read any of those books I wanted to take a quick moment and cover how to open, close, save, and rename an Access database.

Open an Access Database

To start a brand new Access Database, I simply click on Access 2013 from my applications menu or the shortcut I have on my computer's taskbar. This opens a home screen where I can choose "Blank Desktop Database".

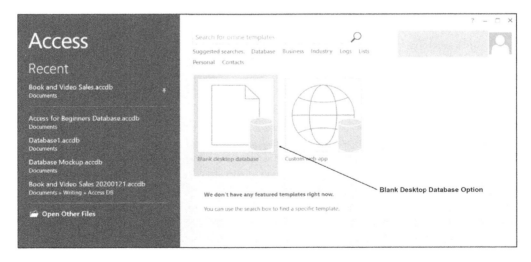

Once you click on that image a dialogue box will appear that allows you to name the database. Type in your name for the database under File Name and then click on the Create button. When you do this, a permanent Access database is created and saved to your computer. (This is different from Word, Excel, and PowerPoint where the file isn't permanently saved anywhere on your computer until you choose to save it.)

If you'd rather work with a template, Access does provide database templates that you can use instead. Click on the Business, Industry, Logs, Lists, Personal, and Contacts options above the database image and it will search online for templates for you. (I have never used one, but they're there and one might be helpful if you're building a database from scratch with no external data source.)

If you're opening an existing Access file, you can either go to the folder where the file is saved and double-click on the file name, open Access and then click on the database name on the left-hand side under Recent, or open Access and then click on Open Other Files and navigate from there to where the database is saved.

You can also, if you're already in a database, go to the File tab at the top of the screen, click on Open, and then choose the database you need that way.

Unlike Excel, Word, and PowerPoint which let you work with more than one file at a time, Access doesn't let you work in more than one database at a time. If you open a new database it closes the one you were already in.

Also, when you attempt to open a recently-created database Access may display "SECURITY WARNING: Some active content has been disabled. Click for more details" when the file is reopened. You don't need to enable that content to see your data, but it means that the database may not be fully functional because certain types of queries or certain macros may not run.

However, to have your database fully functional you do need to click on Enable Content.

This is a good time to remind you to be sure when opening an Access database created by someone else that you trust them before you click on that option. I have vague recollections of hearing about Access databases that were used to distribute malware or something like that. To the point that I wouldn't willingly open an Access database that didn't come to me through a trusted source.

Save an Access Database

In general, you don't have to save an Access database the way you do a Word, Excel, or PowerPoint file. As soon as you make an edit to any of your data, it automatically saves.

I will note here, though, that while you don't have to save the entire database you will need to save any changes you make to queries, reports, or forms as well as to the formatting of your tables.

Access will remind you of this when you close the table, query, report, or form. A dialogue box will appear asking if you want to save your changes. Click yes or no.

You do still have the Save As option for a database, however, which you can use when you want to save a copy of the database under a new name or in a new location. To do that, go to the File tab, choose Save As, select your database type (I always choose Access Database), and then click on the Save As button.

This will bring up the Save As dialogue box where you can choose your location and specify the new database name as needed.

Keep in mind that some older versions of Access may not be able to open a database saved under a newer format.

Delete an Access Database

You can't delete an Access database from within Access. You'll need to navigate to the folder where the database is stored and delete the database there without opening it. (You also can't have it open in Access while trying to delete it.)

Click on the file name to select it and then choose Delete from the menu at the top of the screen, or right-click and choose Delete from the dropdown menu.

Rename an Access Database

There are two ways to create a version of your Access database with a new name.

First, you can Save As and choose a new name for the database. But that will mean you now have two versions, one with the old name and one with the new name.

Or you can navigate to where you've saved the database, click on the name once to highlight but not open, click on it a second time to highlight the name, and then type in the new name you want to use. If you do it that way, there will only be one version of the file, the one with the name you wanted.

If you do rename a file, know that you can't then access it from the Recent listing under Open file. Even though it might be listed there under the old name, Access won't be able to find it because it no longer has that name. (Same thing happens if you move your Access database from the location it was in when you were last working on it.)

Close an Access Database or Access

To close an Access database that you have open, just click on the X in the top right corner. You can also go to the File tab and choose Close which will keep Access open but close that specific database. Or you can use Alt + F4 to exit Access completely.

BASICS OF NAVIGATING ACCESS

Now let's cover some basics of navigating within Access.

See Objects in the All Access Objects Pane

By default the All Access Objects Pane is visible on the left-hand side of your screen and will list all tables, queries, forms, or reports in the current database. If there are more objects than can be shown on the screen, there will be a scroll bar on the right-hand side of the pane that can be used to scroll downward to see the rest of the available objects.

Collapse An Object Category in the All Access Objects Pane

If you have a large number of objects in the All Access Objects pane, you may want to minimize one type of object (such as tables) to make the rest of the objects visible.

To do so, click on the double upward arrow next to that object type. The individual objects in that category will no longer be shown, you'll just see the category label.

In the image below I've collapsed the Tables category.

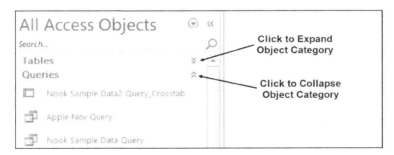

Another way to do this is to right-click on the category name and choose Collapse Group from the dropdown menu.

Expand An Object Category in the All Access Objects Pane

To expand a category that you collapsed, click on the double downward facing arrow next to the category label in the All Access Objects pane. You should now see all objects in that category.

Or you can right-click on the category label and choose Expand Group from the dropdown menu.

Collapse All Categories in the All Access Objects Pane

To collapse all categories at once, right-click on one category name, and choose Collapse All from the dropdown menu.

Expand All Categories in the All Access Objects Pane

To expand all categories at once, right-click on one category name, and choose Expand All from the dropdown menu.

Hide A Category or Object in the All Access Objects Pane

Let me say first, I don't recommend doing this. But someone is bound to want to know how, so let's cover it.

To hide a category of objects, right-click on the category label, and choose Hide from the dropdown menu.

To hide a specific table, query, form, or report, right-click on the object name, and choose Hide in this Group from the dropdown menu.

If the category or object you wanted to hide didn't disappear but was instead just grayed out, see below under Unhide a Category or Object for an explanation.

Unhide a Category or Object in the All Access Objects Pane

The reason I didn't recommend hiding a category or object is because bringing it back is not as straight-forward as you'd want it to be. In Excel I could hide a worksheet and then right-click on any other worksheet and choose Unhide and go from there. That's not how it works in Access.

You have to go to the All Access Objects header and right-click there to see a dropdown menu that includes Navigation Options. Click on that to bring up the Navigation Options dialogue box.

From there you then need to click the box under Display Options that says "Show Hidden Objects". Click OK and go back to your All Access Objects pane.

Your hidden objects will now show but be grayed out like with the ACX table in the image below:

Once you can see your hidden object, you can then right-click on the hidden category label or hidden object, and choose Unhide or Unhide in this Group, as the case may be.

Note that once you change that display setting it will remain changed until you change it again. So if you then hide another object that object will not be hidden, it will just be grayed out, until you go back into Navigation Options and uncheck the box to show hidden objects.

Rename a Table, Query, Form, or Report in the All Access Objects Pane

To rename any object, right-click on its name in the All Access Objects pane and choose Rename from the dropdown menu. That will allow you to type a new name into the white bar where the current name is.

Delete a Table, Query, Form, or Report in the All Access Objects Pane

First, let me just caution you that once you're actively using a database I'd advise against deleting an existing data table or query unless you know absolutely that it is not used anywhere and is not needed.

I do have to delete tables or queries that I've just created, so I use this often. But if I have a table or query that's been sitting in my database for a long time, I usually leave it alone because it may be used somewhere important and I'd rather it sat there than that I broke a report by deleting it.

To delete an object, right-click on its name in the All Access Objects pane, and choose Delete from the dropdown menu. When Access asks if you're sure you want to do that, say OK.

Your other option is to click onto the object name in the All Access Objects pane and choose Delete from the Records section of the Home tab.

Open a Table, Query, Form, or Report from the All Access Objects Pane

Once you've created a table, query, form, or report it will show in the All Access Objects pane that is visible by default on the left-hand side of the screen.

To open a specific table, query, form, or report, double-click on its name.

The contents of that table, query, form, or report will now be visible in the main workspace. Note that you can have more than one of these objects open at the same time.

Navigating Between Multiple Open Tables, Queries, Forms or Reports

When you have more than one table, query, form, or report open at once you can see this because each one will show as a tab in your workspace with the name of the object on the top of the tab. The one you currently have open will be bolded like below with Nook Sample Data Query.

Nook Sample Data	Nook Sample Data Query	Table1 Form	Table1 Report
Date of Sale	Title	Net Units Sol	Total Royalty	Vendor

Date of Sale	Title	Net Units Sol	Total Royalty	Vendor
8/1/2017	A Title	1	0.12345656	Nook
8/2/2017	A Title	1	0	Nook
8/3/2017	A Title	1	0	Nook
8/6/2017	A Title	1	0	Nook
8/10/2017	A Title	1	0	Nook
				Nook

To move to another open object, just click on its tab.

Close an Open Table, Query, Form, or Report

To close an open table, query, form, or report, right-click on the tab for that object and select Close from the dropdown menu. If you want to close all open objects at once, choose Close All from the dropdown.

You can also click on the X in the far right-hand corner of the workspace to close the currently selected object.

Moving Within A Table or Query in Datasheet View

Datasheet view is the default view for tables and queries and when you're in that view they look very much like an Excel worksheet with a series of columns and rows.

You can click into any one of the entries in a table or query and then use either the arrow keys or the Tab and Shift + Tab keys to move around to other entries.

Also, the scroll bars can be used to change the information that's visible in the workspace.

You can also use the Record navigation options at the bottom of the workspace, but since arrowing to the next record will literally just move you down one single row, I don't use it often. Clicking on the arrow with a bar at the end will quickly move you to the end of the data or the top of the data, though.

Moving Within a Form in Form View

The default view for forms is Form View. For a specific record, click into an entry and then use Tab and Shift + Tab to move between entries on the form. If your form is set up such that there is one page per entry, then you can use the navigation options at the bottom of the workspace to move to other records.

Record: ⏮ ◄ 1 of 160 ► ⏭ ►

You can type a record number into the white space (that says of 1 of 160 in the screenshot above) to move to a specific record. Note that this is based on the relative position of the record in your overall list. It is not based on the ID of the record if there is an ID field.

You can also use the single arrows to move forward or backward one record at a time. And the arrows that are pointing at a line to move to the first record or the last record, depending on the direction of the arrow. Arrows are only dark when they're available for use. If they're grayed out that's because you're likely on the first or last record already.

Moving Within a Report

The default view for reports is Report View. You can technically use the Tab and Shift + Tab keys to move from one entry in a report to another, but there's honestly not much point to it because you can't change the values anyway and they're easier to read when you don't have them selected.

The scroll bars on the right-hand side or on the bottom of the workspace will let you see all of the data contained in your report.

If your report is in Print Preview, then you will have the page navigation options at the bottom of the screen as discussed above for forms where, in this case, a single arrow will move you one printed page at a time.

* * *

Okay. So those were some absolute basics for working with Access. Now let's talk about tables. I'm going to do this a little backwards from how probably anyone else would approach this by starting with how to upload an existing Excel file to create a table rather than how to create a table from within Access.

TABLES:
PREPARING AN EXTERNAL DATA SOURCE

The way I use Access is based largely upon bringing external data sources into my database, so almost all of my tables are created by uploading an existing data file and then appending additional data to that table over time from external data files.

For me this is primarily .csv files or Excel files. You can upload other types of files, like text files or .XML, but for this book all we're going to cover is .csv and .xls or .xlsx files.

Preparing Your Data

The first step in uploading a data file from another source is to prepare that file for upload.

First, save a copy of the original file somewhere so that you always have an original version of the file as it existed before you made your changes. That way you can always start over if needed.

Now, open your file because we need to see if the data in the file is ready for upload.

Here, for example, is a mock-up of what the file I receive from Barnes & Noble looks like.

	A	B	C	D	E	F	G	H	I	J	K	L	M	N	O	P	Q
1	Date of Sale	Date of e	B&N Identif	Publisher'	Title	Publisher	Country o	Currency	List Price	Currency	Unit Roya	Units Sold	Units Ret	Net Units	Currency	Total Royalty	
2	8/1/2017		123456789		A Title	An Author	US	USD		0 USD	0	1	0	1 USD		0	
3	8/2/2017		123456789		A Title	An Author	US	USD		0 USD	0	1	0	1 USD		0	
4	8/3/2017		123456789		A Title	An Author	US	USD		0 USD	0	1	0	1 USD		0	
5	8/6/2017		123456789		A Title	An Author	US	USD		0 USD	0	1	0	1 USD		0	
6	8/10/2017		123456789		A Title	An Author	US	USD		0 USD	0	1	0	1 USD		0	
7	Total (Net) Ur	Total Revenue: 0.00															
8																	
9																	

It's almost there.

The first row contains labels for each column, there are no summary columns on the right-hand side, and no subtotals within the data. Also, every row of data represents a complete record. Information for a single transaction is stored on a single row.

The only tweak that needs to be made here is that I need to delete the summary row at the bottom. (In Row 7.)

Here's a mockup of what Amazon used to send me:

	A	B	C	D	E	F	G
1	Title	Author	ASIN	Units Sold	Units Refunded	Net Units Sold or KENP Read**[1]	Royalty Type[2]
2							
3	Sales report for the period 01-Aug-2016 to 31-Aug-2016						
4	Amazon Kindle US Store						
5	A Book	An Author	B123234	1	0	1	70%
6	A Book	An Author	B123234	1	0	1	70%
7	Total Royalty for sales on Amazon Kindle US Store (USD)						
8							
9	Title	Author	ASIN	Units Sold	Units Refunded	Net Units Sold or KENP Read**[1]	Royalty Type[2]
10							
11	Sales report for the period 01-Aug-2016 to 31-Aug-2016						
12	Amazon Kindle UK Store						
13	A Book	An Author	B123234	1	0	1	70%
14							
15							
16	Title	Author	ASIN	Units Sold	Units Refunded	Net Units Sold or KENP Read**[1]	Royalty Type[2]
17							
18	Sales report for the period 01-Aug-2016 to 31-Aug-2016						
19	Amazon Kindle DE Store						
20	There were no sales during this period						

This one is a hot mess. (They've fortunately gotten their act together in recent years.)

The first row is good. We have labels for each column of data.

But then there's a random blank row. And two additional rows of text that set off the first set of data which is for the US store.

Unfortunately, you need the information in that third row that tells you the store where the sales occurred, so not all information is contained in a single row for each transaction.

Rows 5 and 6 have sales information in them. That's what we need for our import.

But then Row 7 is a summary row for that first section and we repeat the whole mess again for the next store.

This report requires a ton of manual work to get the data you actually want extracted from the garbage they surround it with. (I suspect that's because this was created as a final report and not something anyone expected to be used elsewhere. If you have control over your data source, always try to get as close to the raw data file as you can because a report with summaries and pretty headings and extra rows is a pain to work with. I discuss issues like that in far more detail in *Data Principles for Beginners* if it's something you need to know.)

Okay.

So what you ideally want is just the raw data and nothing else. The first row should be the labels you want for each column and then your data should be listed in rows below that without any gaps or any summaries below, within, or off to the side of the data. And all information for each transaction/record should be on one single row. You shouldn't have to look to a different row or file name for necessary information.

If I were creating a file myself, I'd make sure that each column had its own unique name. But when I'm importing from someone else's file, I just leave the column names alone.

I try to change the files I receive as little as I possibly can.

With the Nook file above that's pretty simple. Just delete the summary row (Row 7) and it's done.

With the Amazon file I found it was easier to create a new worksheet. I copied the column headers from Row 1 of the Amazon file, added a column for store at either the beginning or the end, and then copied over the rows of transaction data for each store.

(Shift + Ctrl + arrow down + arrow over is a very hand way to quickly select all of your data in a section and then you can just copy with Ctrl + C and paste with Ctrl + V.)

What I'd get is something like this:

	A	B	C	D	E	F	G	H	I	J	K	L	M	N
1	Store	Title	Author	ASIN	Units Sold	Units Refunded	Net Units Sold or KENP	Royalty Type	Transaction Type	Avg List Price without tax	Avg File Size	Avg Offer Price without tax	Avg Delivery	Royalty
2	US	A Book	An Author	B123234	1	0	1	70%	Standard	4.99	0.20	4.99	0.03	3.47
3	US	A Book	An Author	B123234	1	0	1	70%	Standard	4.99	0.20	4.99	0.03	3.47
4	UK	A Book	An Author	B123234	1	0	1	70%	Standard	3.99	0.20	3.99	0.03	2.79
5														
6														

First row has column labels, then data, no gaps, no summaries.

Once I made all my changes, I'd save the file so it was ready for upload.

Also, ideally, the file you use for upload only has one worksheet in it. (That saves you the step of having to tell Access which worksheet you want.) But if there's more than one worksheet in your file, just be sure you know what it's called so you can select it when the time comes.

TABLES:
UPLOADING AN EXCEL FILE

If the file you saved the data in is an Excel file, then you can use the Excel File upload option.

To do this, go into your Access database, click on the External Data tab, go to the Import & Link section, and click on Excel. This brings up the Get External Data – Excel Spreadsheet dialogue box.

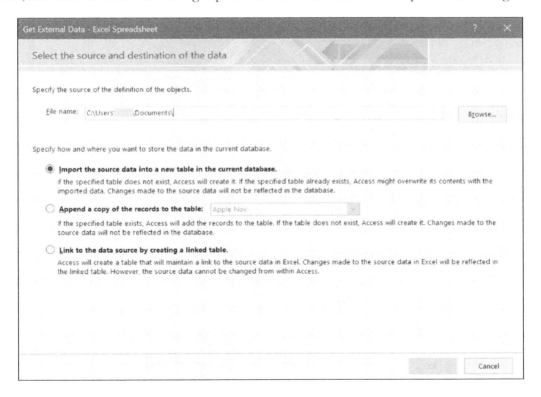

For a new data table, you want to choose the "Import the source data into a new table in the current database" option under where it asks you to "specify how and where you want to store the data in the current database". It will likely already be chosen for you.

(If this is your first table in the database there will only be two choices to choose from. If it's not, there will be three choices like in the image above.)

In the top section where it says "Specify the source of the definition of the objects" and shows a partial file path next to File Name, click on Browse, navigate to where you've saved your source file, click on the file name, and choose Open in the File Open dialogue box.

You should now have the path to that file showing under File Name.

Click OK.

At this point you may see a dialogue box that says "The first row contains some data that can't be used for valid Access field names. In these cases, the wizard will automatically assign the field names."

If that happens, I just click OK.

Chances are if you're uploading a data file that wasn't specifically prepared for use in Access that you'll get this message. Since I prefer to keep the names of the columns as close to the original source as possible, I always just let Access make whatever changes it sees fit. But if you really don't like that then make sure your source file has simple names for each column and that those names do not repeat, do not use weird characters, and do not use reserved column names.

On the next screen, Access will bring up the Import Spreadsheet Wizard dialogue box which will show your data split into columns. There is a box for whether or not the first row of your data contains column headings. Often by default it will be checked, but if it isn't then you should probably check it. If you've set up your data like we discussed previously, then that first row will be your column headings.

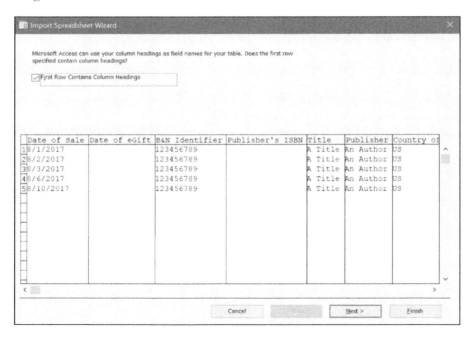

You can see above that my first row has been pulled out of the data and used to label each column in the preview.

To get an idea for how your data is going to look when it imports, scroll to the right or down in the preview section.

Usually I just click right through this screen by choosing Next unless something in the preview looks off.

In the next screen you can choose the format for your data. You can also tell Access not to import that column.

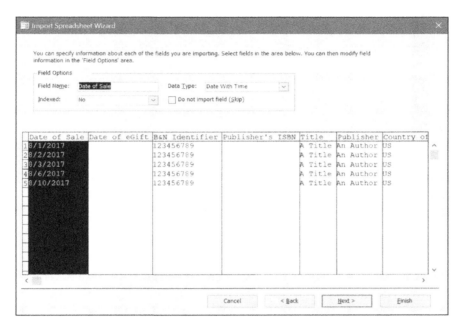

Once again, I usually leave this alone because I'm trying to stay as close to the original source of my data as I can since I know I'll be uploading more data from that source over time and the closer I can stay to the original the less issues I'll have in the future.

But you can click on each column and see the Data Type that Access has chosen for your data. And you can also choose not to import a field. Just know that by doing so you may alter Access's ability to upload more data from that same source in the future.

There are definitely reasons you might want to change the data type that Access initially assigns to a data field, I just prefer to do so elsewhere as the need arises.

However, one field I would check at this point if it were in my data is a zip code field. You do not want Access to treat a zip code as a number because it will drop any 0 at the front of the number. So a zip code of 06314 will become 6314.

Often numbers in Excel files that I receive are formatted as some form of Text already, so it's generally not an issue. The assigned format is more likely to be a problem when uploading a .csv or text file.

In general, though, my default action here is to simply choose Next which then leads to a dialogue box where I can assign a primary key.

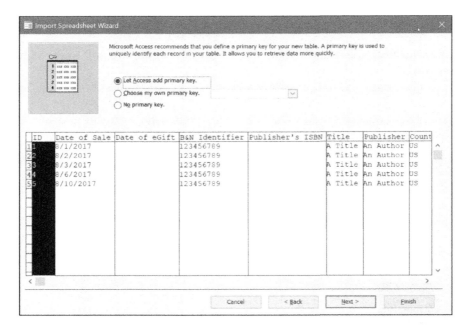

You have three choices for the primary key: let Access add a primary key, choose one of your columns to serve as the primary key, or don't use one at all.

Unless you have a reason for doing so, my recommendation is to just let Access add the primary key. It does put one more column into your data table, labeled ID and will make it the first column, but it ensures that every record in that table is unique.

I personally see no harm in having that column in my tables even though I never use it.

The other option I would recommend is to choose a primary key from the data you're uploading. This is the best option to use when you're bringing in data that has already been set up with a primary key. For example, a customer contact database where every customer has a unique Customer ID. In that case, if you already have a field that contains unique values, might as well use it.

Keep in mind, though, that the values in a primary key field must be unique. So, for example, if you had a column in your table with social security number in it and there was a possibility that you could list a customer twice, say they open two accounts with you, then you couldn't use social security number as a primary key even though a social security number is supposed to be unique to an individual.

Most databases assign their own unique identifiers for this reason, because you can't trust that most of the data you're collecting will in fact be unique.

Honestly, unless the data you're bringing in has already been built with a primary key, I would just let Access create the primary key itself.

I should add here that in more traditional database structures tables are often linked based on the primary key. As we discussed above, Customer ID, Product ID, etc. But that's not how I use Access. Primary keys are something I tend to ignore in my own database.

(We'll come back to this when we build our table relationships.)

Also, even though I don't use them I still wouldn't recommend having no primary key. I don't know why I feel so strongly about it, but I have some sort of gut-level aversion to creating a table of data that doesn't use a primary key.

Okay, then.

Once you've made your primary key decision, click Next again. The next screen allows you to name your table. By default it will usually use the file name but I have also seen it use the worksheet name. If you don't like what it's chosen, click in the name field, and change it.

And then click Finish.

(You'll note on that final screen that you could also check a box to have the wizard analyze your table. I never do this. The only reason to do so is if you're importing a large amount of raw data that you want to split into multiple tables to avoid the duplication of data and aren't sure how to split it or want Access to do that for you. Since I don't use Access that way, I don't use this option. Even if I did, I'm a control freak and probably wouldn't trust Access to know the difference between values that are repetitive and can be split out vs. values that look repetitive but need to remain part of the transaction record.)

Okay.

Once you click on Finish, Access will upload your data and create a table from it.

There is one last dialogue box that asks if you want to save your import steps. I've never seen a reason to do so, so I always say no.

You will now have a new table under the Tables heading in the All Access Objects pane on the left-hand side of the screen. To see what imported, double-click on the table name and you'll see your data in Datasheet View in the main workspace.

There may also be a data table called [TableName]$_ImportErrors where TableName is whatever you chose to name your table. If this happens, not all of your data imported. You can open that table to see what errors occurred in the upload. Sometimes this is proceeded by an error message that not all of your data could be uploaded.

Here is an example of one of these error data tables:

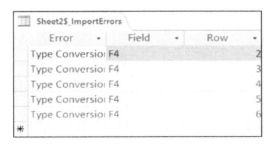

You can see that Access gives you the field name and the row from your Excel file where the import error occurred, as well as telling you what type of error it was.

I see this on a regular basis because one of my vendors provides data with N/A values in certain cells and Access cannot handle an N/A value when the field is a Number field in my Access database. It leaves the field blank. So I usually just tell Access it's fine and to complete the upload.

But with a new data table it's always good to spot check any import errors to make sure crucial information wasn't lost.

Finally, I always open my newly-created table to do a spot check and see if it all looks alright.

Once your data is uploaded to a table you can use that table to build queries, forms, or reports. Or you can add summaries, sort, and filter within the table itself.

So that was Excel. Now let's cover how to upload a .csv file type.

TABLES:
UPLOADING A .CSV FILE

I honestly don't upload .csv files all that often because when I open them in Excel to make sure that there isn't excess information that needs to be fixed I usually end up saving the resulting file as an Excel file.

But you can upload a .csv file, so let's walk through how to do that.

In your Access database go to the External Data tab and click on Text File in the Import & Link section.

The first screen is going to look exactly like the one we saw above with Excel file uploads except it's called the Get External Data – Text File dialogue box. So click on the option to import your source data into a new table and then select the file you want to import using the Browse button.

Note that with both the Excel and the text option, when you navigate to where your file that you want to upload is saved you can only see the files that are in the permitted format. So in this case when I navigate to where I have both an Excel version and a .csv version of my file I can only see the .csv version.

After you've selected your file, click on OK to move to the next screen.

You will now see the Import Text Wizard which is where you tell Access how your data in your .csv file is separated, Delimited or Fixed Width.

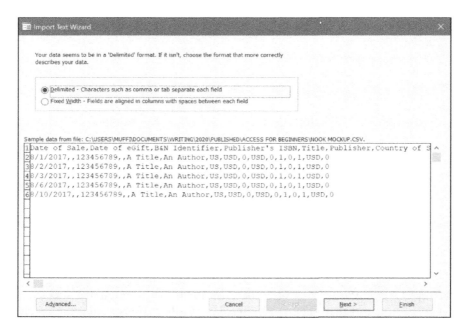

Usually the data will be delimited, meaning it's separated with a tab or a comma or some other identifiable character. Fixed Width data is data that always takes up the same amount of characters for each field.

You can see your data as it looks in the .csv file in the preview section below, but you won't be able to tell whether you chose the right option until you click on Next at the bottom of the page and specify your delimiter or field width on the next screen. Until you do that the data is shown in its raw format.

But in this case we can see that the data is separated by commas so Delimited is going to be the correct choice.

When you choose the Delimited option, the next screen will have you identify what character is being used as your delimiter.

Access does make an attempt to automatically identify the character, so if your data in the preview window looks correct you should be fine.

You can see above that the data has now been split into columns in the preview section and that those columns correctly separate the entries. However, Access did not automatically identify that there was a header row for the data which means I need to check that box that says "First Row Contains Field Names".

(When I did that, Access gave me the same warning message it did with the Excel file that some of my column names weren't suitable as field names and that it would assign them for me. I just said OK.)

If your data was fixed width instead, then this screen would require you to insert lines to show where the breaks in your data should be.

With either option, make sure your data looks "right" in the preview before you click on Next to move to the next screen which is identical to the one with the Excel upload where you can choose to format your data.

Note that Access sometimes will assign a different format to values that are uploaded from a .csv file than it does to that same data that was saved in an Excel file format. For example, for numbers Access used the Double field type when I uploaded this data from Excel but the Long Integer field type when I uploaded from the .csv file.

Either way, as I mentioned before, I tend not to mess with the data choice Access makes at this point in time unless I know that it's made an incorrect choice that could have a long-term impact on my data like setting a zip code field as a number type of field.

When you're done, click Next to make your decision with respect to your primary key.

Click Next again and change your table name if you need to.

Click Finish.

If you're uploading a new table and already have a table by that name in your database, you will get an error message saying so.

If you choose to continue with your import of the new file it will overwrite your existing table. All of that existing data will be lost. So if you get that error message, be very very certain that you want to overwrite whatever data table you already have before clicking Yes.

Chances are, you don't want to do that and would be better off choosing No and then giving the table a different name. You can always delete the old table manually later if you need to.

The final dialogue box you'll see is for saving your import steps, which I never do. Click on Close.

Just like with uploading an Excel file you now have a table that contains your data in the Tables section of the All Access Objects pane.

Note that regardless of the source file type (Excel or .csv), once the information is added into Access it's just a data table. There's no difference in overall structure based on the source file. (Although, as we noted, there can be different data types assigned to specific fields.)

TABLES:
EXPORTING AN EXISTING TABLE TO EXCEL

In the next chapter we'll discuss how to upload additional data to an existing table. My first step when I'm going to do this is to actually export a current copy of the table I'm going to add data to. So I want to walk through that now.

To export a table from Access to Excel, click on the table name, go to the External Data tab, and click on Excel in the Export section.

I always choose "Export Data With Formatting and Layout" and also choose to open the destination file after the export operation is complete.

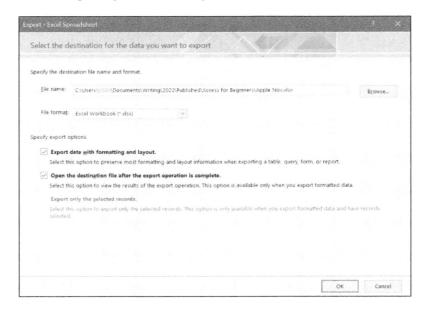

If you don't tell it to open the destination file afterward, you'll just need to go find the file wherever it exported to, which is shown in the File Name box at the top.

Click on OK once you've made your selections. If you chose to open the file, Excel will open and display the data from your table in an Excel worksheet.

There will also be a dialogue box in Access asking if you want to save your export steps. I never do, so I just click on Close. (Access will flash at you in the background until you make that choice, which is kind of annoying. Alt + Tab is a quick way to move back and forth between Access and Excel so you can take care of that.)

TABLES:
UPLOADING DATA TO AN EXISTING TABLE

Because I usually work with outside data sources, the way I add data to an existing table is usually by uploading a new Excel file rather than by manually entering data directly in Access.

The process I use may be more involved than you need, but I find it prevents me from having any significant upload issues so it's the one I prefer.

Once I've established all my data tables in Access and built all my queries and reports that are based off of those tables I will usually export a current version of each data table to Excel. This is because sometimes I change the data type so that I can, for example, do summary calculations on a number field that my vendor initially stored as text. This creates a mismatch between my Access data type for each field and the data type in my vendor reports. I like to fix that mismatch before I upload my files to Access rather than after.

I can easily export my data tables because they are relatively small. If you have very large sets of data, you could use a query that uses all fields from a data table but just a small subset of the records. The goal is to have an Excel file with the exact same columns as your data table and at least one row of formatted data.

Once I have my data table exported to Excel, I delete everything in that Excel file except for the top two rows. The top row gives me my field names. The next row gives me my data formats.

I also delete the ID column if I'm using an AutoNumbered primary key from Access.

As mentioned before, a quick way to select a range of records in Excel is to click in the top left cell of the range that you want (in my case Cell A3), hold down Shift + Ctrl, then use the down arrow and the right arrow to select the entire range. I then use the Delete key to delete the data.

That should leave you with something like this:

	A	B	C	D	E	F	G
1	B&N Identifier	DateSale	Title	Date of eGift	Publisher's ISBN	Country of Sale	Currency
2	123456789	01-Aug-17	A Title			US	USD
3							
4							

If you built your initial table using your external data source as your template, you should now be able to go to that external data source, select the data you need, paste it into this document, and have it match column for column.

(That's why I try not to adjust data even if there are columns I know I don't need. Because if I delete columns in my Access tables then I have to remember to delete those columns again every single time I upload new data from that source.)

When I paste from my vendor reports, I copy and paste the header row as well as the data I want so that I can compare my column headers and make sure that everything lines up.

I paste the information from my source file into the downloaded Excel file starting in Row 4.

I then compare my column headers between the data table from Access and the data that I've just pasted into the document to make sure they match. You can see in this example that I have a problem.

	A	B	C	D	E	F	G
1	**B&N Identifier**	**DateSale**	**Title**	**Date of eGift**	**Publisher's ISBN**	**Country of Sale**	**Currency**
2	123456789	01-Aug-17	A Title			US	USD
3							
4	Date of Sale	Date of eGift	B&N Identifier	Publisher's ISBN	Title	Publisher	Country of Sale
5	8/1/2017		123456789		A Title	An Author	US
6	8/2/2017		123456789		A Title	An Author	US
7	8/3/2017		123456789		A Title	An Author	US
8	8/6/2017		123456789		A Title	An Author	US
9	8/10/2017		123456789		A Title	An Author	US

My column headers from my Access file do not match my column headers from my vendor. That is because between when I uploaded the original data file and now I've reordered the column headers in that table in Access.

I have to fix this or else it will create an issue in my data upload.

At this point I would go back to Access and move my columns around until they match the order from the source file.

(I do that instead of changing the data that I'm importing because the source file is going to continue to be in this order every month. If I don't reorder my Access columns to match it I'll have to fix this issue every month, which is a waste of time. Better to just fix it once in Access than fix it every single month when I go to upload new data.)

No matter how many times I've uploaded data from an existing source, I perform this check to make sure that the new data is aligned with my existing table. This is because every single one of my vendors has changed something in their reports at some point in time without notice. The first I become aware of it is generally when I'm about to upload new data.

Once I've confirmed that my columns match, the next thing I do is Format Sweep from Row 1 (which is the formatting and data type that came from my Access data table) down to the new rows of data that I've just pasted into the table. For me this starts at Row 5, right below the pasted in column names.

(To Format Sweep, select Row 1, click on the Format Painter brush in the Clipboard section of the Home tab, and then select all of your rows of data that you're wanting to sweep that formatting to.)

What this does is makes sure that the data type for the data you're bringing in to Access matches the data type of what you already have there.

Next I delete Rows 2 through 4 which are the old data I kept in Row 2 for its formatting, a blank row, and the header row from the data I'm importing.

That leaves me with a header row in Row 1 that came from Access and so will match my existing table of data followed by all of my new records that I need to import.

I save the Excel file, go back to Access, go to the External Data tab, and click on Excel under the Import & Link section to upload my data.

This brings up the Get External Data – Excel Spreadsheet dialogue box that you've seen before and just like before In the File Name section I use the Browse button to go find the file I want to upload.

(If I didn't get fancy about where it downloaded, it's already going to be in the folder that's showing in the default file path name.)

What is different this time is that I choose the "Append a copy of the records to the table" option instead of choosing to import to a new table.

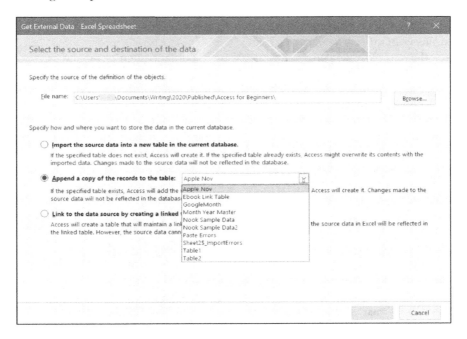

When I click on that option I'm given access to a dropdown menu where I can choose which existing table I want to append the data to.

I choose the table I originally exported from and click OK.

Then I click Next and then Finish to complete the upload steps. (Or really you can probably just click Finish in the second screen.)

Ninety-five times out of a hundred that's all it will take to upload data to an existing table. The data will be added onto the end of the entries that were already there.

I always open the table to confirm that they're there and that they look okay.

* * *

Every once in a while this process does not work.

Usually when it doesn't work I get a "Subscript Out of Range" error message. It's not a helpful error message because it doesn't tell you what you need to fix and doing an internet search for explanations doesn't provide much clarity.

Sometimes it's a formatting mismatch.

Sometimes it seems to be Access seeing columns of data outside of what it expects for that table (even if they're blank).

I think sometimes it can be using a formula and Access not knowing how to handle that formula.

But whatever it is, it's annoying. And often hard to fix.

If you used a formula, you can go to your Excel file, copy all of your data, and then paste special – values back into the worksheet to remove the formulas and keep the values, and then try again.

You can also try downloading the file again and format sweeping to your new data again to make sure that you have the same formatting for all of your entries.

Or you can try deleting a handful of blank columns and blank rows at the edge of the data that you want to upload to remove any excess data that Access may think is there.

But sometimes none of that works.

When that's the case, I upload the data into a new table and then copy and paste all rows from that table into my existing table using Paste-Append.

To do this, be sure to name the worksheet that you're uploading something different from your existing table. Otherwise you may overwrite the existing table. And then go to Excel under Import & Link in the External Data tab, and choose to import the source data into a new table. Leave all column formatting and names alone (because you should've already applied that formatting when you were trying to append this data to the existing table and the column names should already be what's in the table in Access). So just Next, Next, Next, Finish.

This will give you a new data table that has the name you used for the Excel worksheet.

Open that table, use Ctrl + A to select all the records and Ctrl + C to copy them. Open the table where you actually wanted the records to go. Click into a cell in the bottom row of that table. From the Clipboard section of the Home tab, click on the arrow under Paste, and choose Paste Append. Access will tell you you're about to paste X number of records. Tell it OK.

As long as your columns match up between the two tables and have the same data types, you should have no issue with pasting the data over this way.

If the columns don't match you will get a lot of error messages about how you're trying to paste numeric data as text or vice versa. Cancel out as soon as you can, because clearly there is a mismatch between the data you're trying to bring in and the data you already have. To figure out why that is, you'll need to look at both tables in Design View and determine where they don't match. (We'll cover views in a minute, don't worry.) And you'll need to change the data type for one or the other and then try to paste again.

If the copy and paste did work, you can delete the second table that was created when you uploaded the new data. Everything should now be in the original table.

It probably sounds messy. And it is. But it works. And many times I've found it easier to add my data to Access this way than to try and figure out where that error message was coming from.

TABLES:
CREATING ONE FROM SCRATCH

The more traditional way to create a table in a self-contained database is to create it within Access. I'd say I only do this about 5% of the time, but I do need to do it on occasion, so let's quickly walk through how to create a data table in Access.

First, go to the Create tab and choose Table from the Tables section.

This will create for you a basic table with one column/field, ID, and the ability to add additional columns/fields. The second column/field shown says "Click to Add". Left-click on the arrow at the end of the column name to choose the type of field you want it to be. If you're unsure, Short Text is usually a safe choice. (We'll go through field data types in the next chapter.)

Access will add your new column and highlight the name, which for the first field you add will be Field1 so that you can change it. Just type your new column name and hit Enter.

Repeat this process until you have all of your desired columns/fields added to the table.

* * *

To add data into the table just go to the field where you want to type your value and enter it. You can move through your table using the arrow keys or the Tab and Shift + Tab keys.

If you try to enter a value that isn't the same as the format you chose for that column you will get an error message and not be able to enter your value.

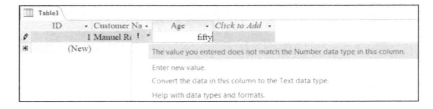

In this case I made the second column a Number data type and then tried to enter my value as text. Access wasn't willing to accept that and told me so. (It will however accept numbers added into a text field since text fields are actually alphanumeric, but those numbers are treated as text and can't be used in calculations.)

* * *

That's it. Pretty easy to add a basic table.

FIELD DATA TYPES

Now we need to talk about the various field data types.

Whether or not you can do something in Access will be driven by the data type assigned to that field. If a field is designated as text, you won't be able to have Access provide you a sum of values in that field, for example. Other data types have limitations on how much text you can enter or on what text you can enter or will convert a number you enter to a whole number, so getting your data types "right" can be important.

The main data types are:

Short Text

(In versions prior to Access 2013 this was referred to as just Text.)

This data type can be used for short, alphanumeric values. This means it can have both numbers and text. The default field size is 255 characters which is about the length of a single paragraph. It's a good choice also for any numeric value that won't be used in calculations, like a phone number. And should be used for numbers where there is a zero in the front, such as zip codes.

Long Text

(In versions prior to Access 2013 this was referred to as Memo.)

Long Text is used for lengthier combinations of text and numbers. It can take up to 63,999 characters. To put this in context, the second paragraph in this chapter is approximately 340 characters long, so think about 175 average-sized paragraphs of text.

AutoNumber

AutoNumber is used for primary keys. It assigns a unique numeric value to the next record (row) in the table. Normally this value will start at 1 and increase by 1 each time. It cannot be updated once assigned and the number also cannot be reused. If you cut a record and paste it back into your table, it will be assigned the next number in sequence.

You *can* change the settings so that Access instead assigns a random unique value to each new record instead of increasing the number by 1 each time. When I did this, the first value it assigned was 846905929 instead of 2. Honestly, I don't think I'd use that setting, but it is there.

Number

Number is the field type to use for numeric values where a mathematical calculation may be performed.

Within the Design View for a table, which we'll talk about next, you can choose different field sizes for the Number field. The most common are Double and Long Integer.

According to Access, you should "use the Long Integer data type when you create a foreign key to relate a field to another table's AutoNumber primary key field."

You can also have Byte, Integer, Single, and Decimal field sizes for Number.

Depending on the size type you choose, there will be limitations. Some, for example, do not allow decimals. And some work in a very narrow range of values.

The following is from the Access Help descriptions for field size.

Byte stores integers from 0 to 255. No fractions/decimals are allowed.

Integer stores integers from -32,768 to 32,767. No fractions/decimals are allowed.

Long Integer stores integers from -2,147,483,648 to 2,147,483,647. No fractions/decimals are allowed.

Decimal stores numbers from -9.999…x 1027 to +9.999…x 1027. (So basically very large numbers in both a negative and a positive direction.) It can be precise up to 28 decimals.

Single stores numeric values with a floating decimal point from -1.797 x 10308 up to 1.797 x 10308. It can be precise up to seven significant digits.

Double stores numeric values with a floating decimal point from -1.797 x 10308 up to 1.797 x 10308. It can be precise up to fifteen significant digits.

Using Number types that take up less storage size requires less memory and can improve processing times. If that's an issue for you, Decimal and Double take up the most storage space. Byte takes up the least.

Currency

The Currency field type is for monetary values and I've also seen Access recommend that it be used for numeric data used in mathematical calculations with up to four decimal places. According to Access it is accurate up to fifteen digits on the left side of the decimal separator.

The reason Access gives for using the Currency type for fields that require many calculations and involve data that has one to four decimal places is that it will calculate faster than the Single and Double data types.

(This is probably a good time to also point out to you the dangers of storing data in more than one currency in your Access database. I don't think Access is really set up to handle that well and if you poke around you'll see that there have been issues for users who try to use the same database but in different geographies. I personally only work in USD in my database which matches to my regional settings. I convert all of my foreign currency values to USD *before* I upload any data to my Access database so that I know that I'm always dealing with values in that one currency and don't have to worry about accidentally combining a Euro value with a USD value without realizing I've done so.)

Date/Time

The Date/Time field provides date and time value for the years 100 through 9999. A Date/Time field can be further formatted in Design View as General Date, Long Date, Medium Date, Short Date, Long Time, Medium Time, and Short Time. Most users will likely prefer Medium Date or Short Date.

Yes/No

The Yes/No data type only allows for one of two values. Those values are by default Yes and No, but can also be set to only accept True/False or On/Off. The field originally shows as a checkbox, but it can be changed to show as text instead by selecting Combo Box under Display Control in the Lookup Tab in the Design View for the table.

* * *

There are also data types for Lookup & Relationship, Rich Text, Attachment, Hyperlink, and Calculated Field but those are more advanced data types that we're not going to cover here.

TABLE VIEWS

The default for viewing a table of data is the Datasheet View. That's the one with your actual data values displayed in rows and columns, like so:

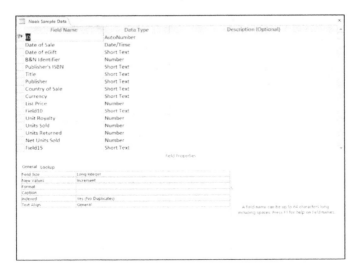

But there is another view available with respect to tables, the Design View. You access this view by going to the Views section of the Home tab, clicking on the dropdown arrow under View, and choosing Design View.

This is what your table of data turns into when you do so:

What you're seeing above is a field listing on the top that has the name, data type, and a description for every single column/field in your data table. This information is listed in rows in this view so your first column is in the first row, your second column is in the second row, etc.

You can see, for example, that the first column in this table is the primary key field that Access added that is labeled as ID and that is set up to be an AutoNumber field. The description for this field is blank, which is the case for all fields by default.

If you are going to have multiple users of your Access database you may want to go through and add a description for key fields so that all users know what information those fields contain. To add a description, just click into the description field for the column you want to describe, type in your description, and hit enter.

Below the column/field listing you can further refine formatting and appearance by using the Field Properties section.

Here, for example, is the default setting for a field that has the Short Text data type:

It's hard to tell, but in this instance I'm clicked into the Field Size field. Off to the right-hand side of the field listing is a description of what that field does. In this case, Field Size determines "the maximum number of characters you can enter in the field." The definition further informs me that 255 is the maximum size I can specify for this field size. (As we discussed above, you can use Long Text if you're going to have more text than that.)

When I choose a field with a Number format, then Field Size becomes a dropdown menu. Like so:

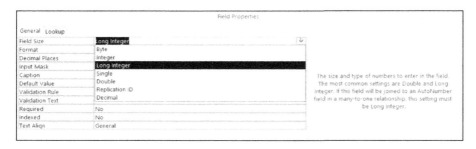

In this case, rather than specify a number of allowed characters, I would specify the Number field size to use. As we discussed above under Field Data Types the different sizes allow for different number lengths and some will not allow decimal places.

* * *

The Field Properties section is also where you can specify a display format for your data, a caption to use in place of the field name, a default value for the field, validation rules to apply when entering data in that field, whether the field must be completed or not for each record, whether to index values in the field, and how to align the text in the field for display purposes.

* * *

This is also the section where you'd go to make your Yes/No checkbox into a text field. Note that there are two tabs in this section. To change your Yes/No checkbox, you'd select the Lookup tab and make your changes there.

* * *

A lot of what I just mentioned are more advanced settings so as a beginner I'd leave them alone as much as you can. Ideally you get your data into your table, let Access format it for you, and then you leave it alone.

But if your data is formatted in a way that doesn't work for you, then you'll need to come here to change it.

The most frequent change I have to make in this view is to take a field that has a numeric value but has been formatted by Access as Short Text and change it to Currency or Number. That's because a large number of my vendors provide numeric data as text by default. (I have this same issue when working in pivot tables in Excel. I often generate a pivot table and set it to Sum and see a result of zero because there's nothing to sum when Excel thinks the entries are text.)

* * *

If size or processing speeds are issues for you, changing these settings can help. But be very careful doing so for an existing database. Access will have to go through and make that change to all of your existing fields, which could hang up or crash your database.

Also, you may lose data if you apply a new format to existing fields. For example, if you have a value of 1.23456 and apply one of the Number formats that don't allow decimals, you'll be left with a value of 1 and that may not be what you want.

If it were me, I'd probably export the data into Excel and make my changes on a copy of it there and then upload to a clean, new database where I assigned the appropriate format as I imported my data.

Just to give you an example of what can happen with one of these changes, I took a Short Text field and put the values "United States" and "US" into fields in a column and then went to the Design View and changed the field size to 2. Access did give me an error message that I'd changed the size of one or more fields to a shorter size, but all it mentioned was that a validation rule might be violated as a result. It didn't mention that I'd lose data.

I went ahead and saved the change, and when I went back to my data table my entry that previously read "United States" was now "Un", and there was no way to undo that change at that point. If I'd done that in a table with thousands of records, imagine how much data I would've lost and been unable to recreate. That "Un" could've been "United Kingdom" just as easily as "United States".

* * *

The other issue with adjusting field size or type is that once you do so, Access will not allow you to input a value that is outside of that range or of a different type. So when my Small Text field allowed 255 characters I could easily type in United States. But the minute I changed it to 2 characters and saved it, I was stuck with just two characters in that field.

So only make those kinds of changes if you are sure you know what you're doing. If you aren't, save a backup of your database before you begin, so you don't lose crucial information if you make a mistake.

* * *

Okay, so that's how the Design View works with respect to tables. I don't use it much with my tables, but I do with queries. Before we talk about those, though, we need to cover how to amend records in tables and how to navigate a table (or query) in Access.

AMENDING RECORDS IN TABLES

Alright. Now that we have a table that we've uploaded into Access or created manually and that table has some data in it, it's time to walk through how to amend the data in your table.

I should note here that most of what we're going to discuss with respect to tables also can apply to certain types of queries, but I would not recommend adding, deleting, copying, cutting, or pasting records in queries since doing so will impact your underlying data table. If you delete a record in a basic detail query, it's deleted from the data table as well. But to be properly in control of what you're doing to your data, I'd make it a habit to always amend data through a table or a form and never through a query even when it's possible to do so.

Okay. So the basics of handling data in an existing table.

Add a New Record To a Table

To add a new record to a table, go to the last row of your table and start typing in your data. There will be a star on the far left side of that row to indicate it's the row where you can add a new record. If the table is using an AutoNumber ID field for its primary key, you will start entering your data in the next column/field over.

If the table is particularly large, just right-click on the gray box on the left-hand side of any existing row/record and choose New Record from the dropdown menu and that will take you to the bottom of the table where you can then add a new record.

Another option is to click anywhere in the table and then choose New from the Records section of the Home tab.

To get to each next field in your row where you're adding your data you can use the Tab or the right arrow key. You can also type in a value in a field and hit Enter and it will move one field over.

If you enter a value in a field that isn't allowed for that field you will get an error message that the value you entered does not match the data type of the column. Choose Enter New Value and type in a value that does work for that field. If you're not sure what will work for the field, delete your current entry, change your view to Design View and see what data type has been assigned to it.

Add a New Field/Column to a Table

To add a new field to your table, right-click on an existing column/field and choose Insert Field. This will insert a new field to the left-hand side of the column you right-clicked on when you chose Insert Field. The field will need to be renamed and you may need to change the Data Type in the Design View screen.

You can also go to the end of the table and click on "Click to Add" on the last column if that's a visible option, and choose the type of new field you want to add from there.

A third option for inserting a new field is to click onto a column/field in your table and go to the Add & Delete section of the Fields tab under Table Tools. Select the Data Type you want, and it will insert a new column/field into the table with that assigned Data Type. The new column will be inserted to the right of the column you were clicked onto in the table.

Move a Field/Column

If a field/column is in your table, but you want to move it to another location in that table, you can do so by holding your mouse over the column name until it becomes a four-sided arrow, like this:

When that happens, left-click and drag the column to where you want it. You'll see a dark black line along the edge of the border between two columns. This dark black line indicates the left-hand side of where the column will be moved to when you release your click. Be sure you drag the column far enough to actually move it, because the first black line you see will likely keep it right where it is.

Rename a Field/Column

To change a field/column name, right-click on the top of the column and choose Rename Field from the dropdown menu. This will highlight the existing field name. Type in the new name you want to use and hit Enter. (You cannot use Undo to reverse this change once you've made it.)

You can also go to Design View, click into the cell for that column under Field Name, and change it there. You'll need to save your change to the table before you can return to Datasheet View and have the new column name take effect.

Delete a Record From a Table

To delete a record from a table, right-click on the gray box on the far left-hand side of the row where that record is stored and choose Delete Record from the dropdown menu.

You can also select the record and then use the Delete option in the Records section of the Home tab.

Access will present you with a dialogue box that says "You are about to delete 1 record(s). If you click Yes, you won't be able to undo this Delete operation. Are you sure you want to delete these records?" Click on Yes if you are. Click on No if you don't want to delete the record after all.

Delete a Column/Field From a Table

To delete a column from a table, right-click on its name to see the columns/fields dropdown menu, and choose Delete Field.

You can also select the column by left-clicking on its name, and then use the Delete option in the Records section of the Home tab or use the Delete option in the Add & Delete section of the Field tab under Table Tools.

Access will ask if you're sure you want to delete the selected records. Say yes if you are.

Cut a Record From a Table

If instead of deleting a record from a table you want to remove the record from the table but have it available to paste into a different table, you can Cut the record. Right-click on the gray box at the left-hand side of the row and choose Cut from the dropdown menu.

You can also select the row and then use Ctrl + X to cut. Or use the Cut option in the Clipboard section of the Home tab.

Whichever way you do it, Access will present you with a dialogue box asking if you want to delete the record. Choose Yes if you want to proceed. In the case of cutting a record, it is actually not yet deleted. You can paste it back into the existing table or a new one. However, keep in mind that you will change the record number if you're using AutoNumbering to assign an ID to your records. Even though it's the same information Access will treat it like a new record.

Cut a Column From a Table

I generally don't recommend cutting a column from a table, but if you need to do so highlight the column by left-clicking on its name and then choose Cut from the Clipboard section of the Home tab. (Cut is not an option in the dropdown menu for columns.)

Copy a Record From a Table

To leave a current record where it is but take a copy of the record to paste elsewhere, highlight the record (by clicking on the gray box on the left-hand side), and then either (a) right-click and choose Copy, (b) use Ctrl + C, or (c) use the Copy option in the Clipboard section of the Home tab.

Copy a Column From a Table

To leave a current column of data where it is but take a copy of the column to paste elsewhere, highlight the column by left-clicking on its name, and then either (a) right-click and choose Copy, (b) use Ctrl + C, or (c) use the Copy option in the Clipboard section of the Home tab.

Paste a Record Into a Table

To paste a record you copied or cut from an existing table into another table, go to the bottom of that new table where there's a row with a star on the left-hand side, click on that row, and then either (a) right-click and choose Paste, (b) use Ctrl + V, or (c) use the Paste or Paste Append option from the Paste dropdown menu in the Clipboard section of the Home tab.

Be careful when doing so that it makes sense. Access will paste in as much of your information as it can as long as the data types of the fields match, but there's no evaluation by Access that the data you're pasting in actually matches the table where it's being pasted into.

Paste Data Into a Column In a Table

If you're overwriting data in an existing column, then copy or cut and paste are pretty simple. You just highlight the column where you want to paste your copied or cut data and then either (a) right-click and choose Paste, (b) use Ctrl + V, or (c) use the Paste option from the Clipboard section of the Home tab.

But when you've cut or copied data and are trying to put it into a new column, you have to create that column first. Only then you can paste your data into that newly created column. Note that the column name will not copy over, just the data. (This is honestly something I'd probably do in Excel rather than Access if it were me. Access started to act a little weird on me when I was cutting and pasting columns, because that's not really something you should be doing on a normal basis.)

NAVIGATING A TABLE OR QUERY IN ACCESS

What we just covered was how to add, delete, or amend records in Access and I recommended that you only do that in your data tables, not your queries. But now let's discuss basic tools for navigating a table or query since these tricks apply to both of them equally.

Select All Data

To select all of the records in your table or query, use Ctrl + A.

You can also go to the Find section of the Home tab and choose Select All from the Select dropdown menu.

(Select All is the easiest way to choose all of the data in a table if you want to copy or cut all rows in that table to paste into another table. As discussed above, I use this when new data I wanted to upload to a table wouldn't upload directly to the table and I have to upload it into a new table and then copy and paste it to the table where I actually wanted it to go.)

Select Multiple Records/Rows

To select more than one row/record in a table, left-click on the gray square to the left side of the topmost row or bottommost row of the range you want to select, and then drag your cursor either downward or upward until all of the rows you want to select are highlighted.

Selecting multiple rows/records only works if they are contiguous (touching one another, in sequential order). Unlike in Excel you can't use the Control key to select multiple rows/records that are not touching.

Select Multiple Columns/Fields

To select more than one column at a time the columns must be side-by-side. Left-click on the name of the left-most or right-most column and then drag your cursor either to the left or the right until all of the columns you want to select are highlighted.

Change the Height of a Row

To change the height of a row, you can hold your mouse over the line between that row and the one below it until the cursor turns into a line with an arrow pointing upward and an arrow pointing downward. Left-click and drag to your desired row height. (Note that I was not able to use Undo to reverse this after I did it.)

You can also select a row and then choose Row Height from the dropdown menu and then either enter a desired value for the height or click the box for standard height to revert your row back to the standard row height used by Access.

Finally, you can go to the Records section of the Home tab, click on the arrow under More, and choose Row Height from there which will also bring up the Row Height dialogue box.

Note that changing the row height for one row will change the row height for all rows in the table. There is no way to change the row height for a single row.

(Another reason it's a good idea to use forms for inputting or reviewing data that can but doesn't have to involve large amounts of text.)

Change the Width of a Column

To change the width of a column, you can hold your mouse over the line between that column and the one to its right until the cursor turns into a line with an arrow pointing to the left and an arrow pointing to the right. Left-click and drag to your desired column width. (Note that I was not able to use Undo to reverse this after I did it.)

You can also select the column, right-click, and then choose Field Width from the dropdown menu to bring up the Column Width dialogue box. From there you can enter the value you want or click the box to change the width to the standard column width.

Finally, you can go to the Records section of the Home tab, click on the arrow under More, and choose Field Width from there to bring up the Column Width dialogue box.

Unlike with rows where changing the height of one row changes them all whether you have them selected or not, with columns only those that were selected will change.

Hide a Field/Column

You can hide a field or fields by right-clicking on the top of the selected columns and choosing Hide Fields from the dropdown menu.

You can also do so by selected the columns you want to hide and then choosing Hide Fields from the dropdown menu under More in the Records section of the Home tab.

Unhide a Field/Column

To unhide a previously hidden field or fields, right-click on the top of any column and choose Unhide Fields from the dropdown menu. This will bring up the Unhide Columns dialogue box. Any field name that isn't checked is currently hidden. Place a check in the box for any field you want displayed.

You can also at the same time remove the check from any box to hide a field/column that's currently visible.

The Unhide Fields option is also available from the More dropdown menu in the Records section of the Home tab.

Freeze Fields/Columns

If you have a table where not all columns of data are visible on the screen, you may find yourself wanting to make sure that certain columns stay visible as you scroll to the right to see the rest of your data.

To "freeze" those columns you want to have remain visible, select the columns, right-click, and choose Freeze Fields from the dropdown menu. The columns/fields you chose to freeze will move to the left-hand side of the table and will remain visible as you scroll to the right.

You can freeze columns one at a time or as a group. If you freeze them one at a time, the order in which you freeze the columns will impact the order in which they are displayed.

In a table, it appears that each field you freeze will be moved to the left-hand side of the table but placed to the right of any previously frozen fields. In a query it appears that each new field you freeze will be moved to the far left-hand side of the query data table. So they work differently.

Another way to freeze your fields/columns is to select the fields, go to the Records section of the Home tab, click on the arrow under More, and choose Freeze Fields from the dropdown menu there.

While I like Freeze Fields, you do need to be careful in using it because if you later choose to unfreeze your columns, that new column order will remain. So if you're going to be uploading additional data to a table from an external source I would suggest that you not use the Freeze Fields option on that table. (Remember when I showed you I had a mismatch between my Access table and my source table in the Uploading Data to an Existing Table chapter? That's what caused it.)

Unfreeze Fields/Columns

To unfreeze your fields/columns, simply right-click on any column in the table and choose Unfreeze All Fields from the dropdown menu.

You can also go to the Records section of the Home tab, click on the arrow under More, and choose Unfreeze All Fields from there. With this option you can be clicked anywhere in the table, you don't have to right-click on a column header first.

QUERIES:
BASIC DETAIL QUERY

Now that you know how to create and work with tables, let's discuss how to create queries.

The most basic type of query involves a single data source (either a data table or a query) and pulls in information from that source without attempting to further summarize or analyze that information. This is the type of query where you can still amend a record and have it impact the underlying data table.

The reason you might create a query like this is to, for example, pull in only a subset of the columns/fields from the original source. You could also combine this type of query with a criteria that narrows down the results to just a subset of the records in the original table, like all customer transactions from 2019.

For all queries, I use the Query Wizard.

(From here on out I'm just going to talk about doing this with a table as the source, but it can be done with another query as well.)

We'll start with this simple type and then we'll work our way up to more complex types later. This is the most basic form of what's called a Select Query.

Okay. Let's create one.

First, click on the table you want to use to build your query.

Then go to the Queries section of the Create tab and click on the Query Wizard. This will bring up a New Query dialogue box.

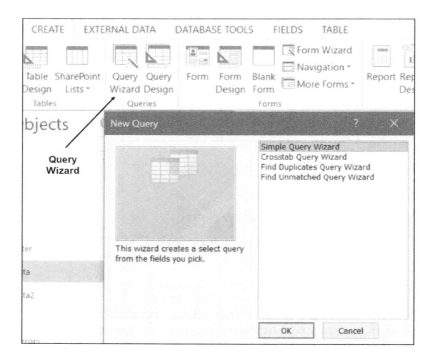

For this type of query you want to choose the Simple Query Wizard. (Actually, in this book that's the only type of query we're going to cover.)

Click on that query type and then click on OK.

You will now see a screen that has a dropdown menu on the left-hand side towards the top of the dialogue box which should show the table you clicked on before you opened the Query Wizard. You can use the dropdown to change your table selection if you chose the wrong one. The dropdown lists all of your data tables and queries, in that order, with all tables listed first followed by all queries.

Below that on the left-hand side is a listing of Available Fields from the table/query that's shown in the dropdown.

The right-hand side which shows your Selected Fields will be blank when you start because you haven't yet selected any fields to include in your query.

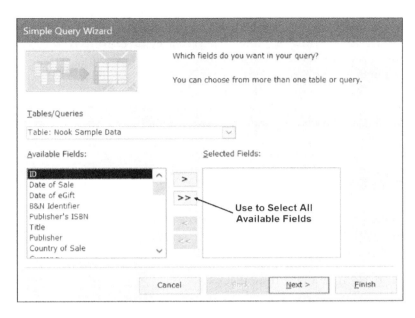

If you want all of the fields from your chosen data source, you can use the double right-hand arrow in between the Available Fields and Selected Fields boxes.

If you just want specific fields, then click on the name of each one you want, in the order you want them, and use the single right-hand arrow. When you do so, those fields you chose will now show in the Selected Fields box and will no longer be shown in the Available Fields box.

Here I've selected four fields that I want in my query:

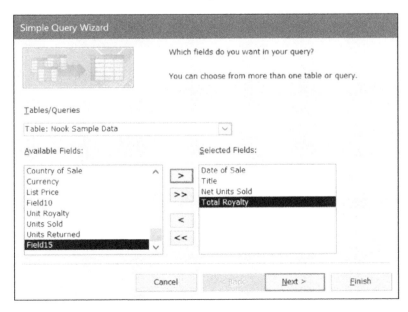

If you decide that you don't want one of the fields you've selected, you can remove all selected fields by using the double left-hand arrow or you can remove a single field from your selection by clicking on its name and then using the single left-hand arrow.

Once you have the fields you want selected, click Next.

You will now have the choice of whether the query should be a Detail query or a Summary query. Because in this instance we just want to bring over our data as it exists now, we're going to leave Detail selected. (We'll walk through a Summary query in a minute.)

Click Next.

Now you have an opportunity to rename the query to something useful to you. Otherwise it will take the name of the table it was derived from and add query on the end. (You can also always rename a query later.) If you don't like the name and want to change it now, change the text in the white box to what you want.

Leave "Open the Query to View Information" checked so that you can see your data.

Click on Finish.

You should now see a new query on the left-hand side in your All Access Objects pane and it should be open in your main workspace and displaying the columns/fields you selected from your data source along with the data pulled from that source.

Because we didn't impose any additional criteria or try to place a summary on the data, it should be the exact same number of rows as the source data. Also, because there's nothing to distinguish this query from the source table, you can actually edit it like you would a table. Any edits made will also be reflected in that original table. But like I said before, I don't recommend doing that.

Alright, now let's create a Summary Query instead.

QUERIES:
BASIC SUMMARY QUERY

We're still only working with one table here, but this time we're going to get Access to summarize our data for us.

This is the data we're working with:

Note that we have entries for three different titles in this table. I want to generate a report that gives me the same information as this report, but I want it grouped by title. Which means I can either group on B&N Identifier or Title because in this case they are unique and tied together.

So. I do the same as before. I click on my table and then choose Query Wizard from the Queries section of the Create tab.

From there I choose Simple Query Wizard and click on OK.

In the next screen I'm going to choose my three data fields that I want to use, Title, Net Units Sold, and Royalty. (Note here that I'm using a slightly different data table than I did in the last example so don't expect them to match.) Once I have my fields, I click on Next.

This is where things deviate from the Basic Detail Query. Now we click on "Summary" instead and then click on the gray button that says Summary Options.

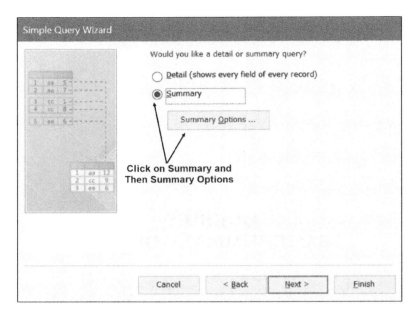

This brings up a separate dialogue box called Summary Options. That box lists each selected field that looks like it can be treated as a number and gives the option of calculating the Sum, Average, Minimum, or Maximum for each of those numbers.

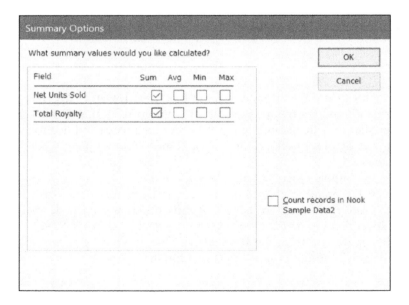

In this case I wanted to Sum both the Net Units Sold and the Total Royalty so I check that box for each one and then choose OK.

From there it's the same as before. The next screen is where you can change the name of the query and choose Finish.

But this is what the result looks like because we wanted summary data and not detail data:

Title	Sum Of Net L	Sum Of Total
A Third Title	2	7.77
A Title	11	21.99
Another Title	1	2.56

Instead of my original ten detailed entries, I now have just three rows of data, one per title, and the values shown in the next two columns are summary values for each of those titles.

A basic summary query like this can be very handy when you have a lot of individual entries and you want to see results at a higher level.

Note also that with this type of query, because it's not a one-to-one tie between the original source table and the query, that you can't modify the results in the query. The option to add or delete a record is grayed out and you can't edit any of the entries.

QUERY VIEWS AND THE DESIGN VIEW

This is a good point in time to stop and talk about your available query views.

To change your view, go to the Views section of the Home tab, click on the arrow under View, and choose the view you want.

You have three choices. One is the one we're in now, the Datasheet View. That's the default view where you can see your actual results.

The next one, the SQL View, is one you aren't going to use at this level of knowledge. It basically lets you use SQL to create a query. Unless you're already familiar with SQL, you're probably just going to leave that alone. (Although in Intermediate Access I will show you how to use what's stored there to create a basic Union Query.)

The final view, Design View, is one I do use often and you will probably use as well.

This is what the table we were just looking at looks like in Design View.

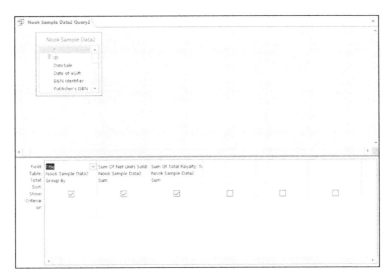

The top half of the display shows you the tables that you're currently using for that query. In this case, we just had the one so that's all that shows. (We'll walk through an example with multiple tables in a minute.)

You can see the table name and then the fields that are available in that table. There's a scroll bar on the right-hand side of that box because there are more fields than are currently visible.

The bottom half of the display shows which fields have been selected for inclusion in the current query and how they're being used.

The first row in that bottom section lists the field/column name. Note that the name Access assigns to those second two columns has been changed. Since we're summing the values it names those columns "Sum of [X]" where X is the original column name. If you want to change the field name, replace the text to the left of the colon or, if there isn't a colon, you can add text then a colon to the left of the text that is currently displayed.

The second row is the name that field/column is being pulled from.

The third row is how that field is being used. In this case we have one field that's being used to Group our data, Title, and two fields that are being used to create summed values.

In addition to Group and Sum there are many other options available for how to use a field.

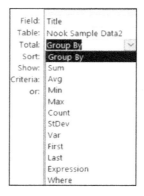

In general I use Group, Sum, Min, Max, and Expression. (Expression is for when you build a formula to make a calculation. That's covered in *Intermediate Access*.)

Below that is a row where you can specify how to sort the data in the query.

After that is a check box so that you can specify whether to include that field/column in the data table that's displayed with respect to that query. (You may at some point in time want to use a field to select certain data but then not have that field display in your query.)

Finally, there's a section where you can add Criteria to apply to your field when creating the query. For example, you could specify that only values greater than zero be included or that only customers in Colorado be included. This is where you'd do that or where that would show. (We'll cover the basics of Criteria later.)

Also. When you have the Design View open there may also be a Property Sheet pane visible on the right-hand side of the screen. If it isn't visible you can go to the Design tab under Query Tools and click on Property Sheet in the Show/Hide section.

Property Sheet ✕

Selection type: Field Properties

General Lookup

Description	
Format	
Input Mask	
Caption	
Text Format	

This gives you the ability to specify a Description, Format, Input Mask, or Caption for each field. For numeric fields you also have a Decimal Places option.

There are two main reasons I use the Property Sheet.

The first is to apply a format to my numbered data. So, for example, in this query the third column is royalties which is a currency amount. I can go to Format, click in that box to show a dropdown arrow, and choose Currency from the list. I can then go to Decimal Places and specify how many decimal places I want shown in my query data table.

(This is very useful when you have data that has a lot of decimal places in it and where you don't care about the value to that level of precision. Without limiting the number of decimal places your value may show in Datasheet View as a series of pound signs #########.)

The second reason I use the Property Sheet is to change the displayed column name for summed values.

As I mentioned above, when you summarize data in Access it by default shows it as Sum of [X] where X is the field you were summarizing. So here we have Sum of Net Units Sold and Sum of Total Royalty when I'd rather the columns were labeled Net Units Sold and Royalty. You can change how this displays by entering a Caption in the Property Sheet.

Another, and probably better, way to do this is to change the rename the column altogether as I discussed above So replace the text before the : in the field name row in Design View with what you want the column name to be.

It may be a little hard to see but I've done this for the second column below. I changed the Field name from "Sum of Net Units Sold: Net Units Sold" to "Net Units Sold: Net Units Sold". That told Access to give that column the name "Net Units Sold" when it displays the table. I've also left the third column Field name unchanged. It's still "Sum of Total Royalty: Total Royalty" but added a caption, "Royalty" on the Property Sheet on the right-hand side of the screen.

Both of those changes have the same impact on the query when it displays in Datasheet View.

Nook Sample Data2 Query2		
Title	Net Units Sold	Royalty
A Third Title	2	7.77
A Title	11	21.99
Another Title	1	2.56

The column names are now what I specified in that view.

The difference between the two approaches is that the one where I used Caption will still use the Access-assigned field name in any other query or report. That can get messy and convoluted over time as you build queries off of queries.

I've always done it that way because I tend not to like to mess with things unless I have to and changing the name like I did with the Net Units Sold column does lose some information and can make back-tracking where a number came from more of a challenge.

But it definitely creates a cleaner name to work with in other queries. And, for the most part, Access will carry any change you make like this through to all of your other queries and reports that use that field without you having to do anything.

As I was writing this book and *Intermediate Access* I decided to go through all of my queries and change the column names permanently rather than use the Caption field since I do have queries of queries of queries. What I noted was that there were three places that those changes did not carry through automatically. All three relate to items we're not covering in this book, but I'll mention them just in case.

One was in any calculations I had in the query where I was making the change. So if I was using that now-renamed field for a calculation I had to change the calculation as well. The second was in any summary rows I had in a report. It showed the values in detail cells fine, but kept the old text for any summary rows. And the third was in some of my union queries where I hadn't copied and pasted the SQL language direct from the source table but had instead written the SQL language myself.

Bottom line: While permanently changing the name of a query column certainly makes it more intelligible and easier to use for other queries or reports, if you're dealing with an active Access database you need to go through and make sure that you haven't broken any queries or reports by doing so. And be aware that if you suddenly get a parameter dialogue box asking for a value that it was probably caused by that change. But we'll cover this again in *Intermediate Access*.

* * *

When you make changes to a query like we did here with changing the column/field names and adding formatting and captions, Access will ask when you close the query if you want to save changes to the design. In this case, unless you were just playing around, always say Yes.

RELATIONSHIPS

Next we're going to explore how to link data from two separate tables or queries to create a query that combines information from both of them. But first we need to discuss relationships, because if you don't tell Access how your tables and queries are related, you can't pull information from more than one at a time.

This is a snapshot of some of the relationships that exist in my current Access database:

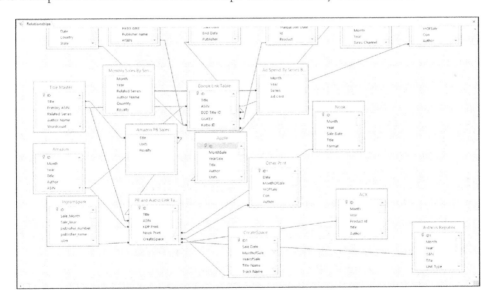

It looks insane, right? I mean, there are lines going every which way. But keep in mind this is something that has built up one relationship at a time over months if not years.

It looks so involved, because for almost every query I create—and I have over a hundred of them—I have to have relationships established between the tables and queries I'm going to use in order to create that query.

But when you're just starting out it is much, much simpler.

So let's walk through how to do this.

First, go to the Database Tools tab and click on Relationships from the Relationships section.

This will bring up a Show Table dialogue box which lists all of your tables and queries.

Select the tables or queries you want to link and then choose Add. (To select more than one table at a time, use Ctrl before you click on the second one, or you can add them individually.)

The tables or queries you selected will now show in your workspace.

Close the dialogue box.

If you realize after you close the dialogue box that you actually wanted to add another table or query, you can right-click in the workspace and choose Show Table from the dropdown menu to bring it back.

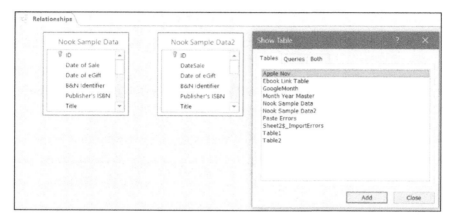

At this point there is not a relationship between the tables or queries you've selected. Access doesn't know how they relate to one another. They're just sitting there.

In this sample here I've chosen two tables that are pretty much identical in terms of their field names. Usually that won't be the case. You'll have one or two fields that overlap between the tables that you'll be using to link on, like ID or Title or Name, but the rest of the table or query will contain unique information. (Otherwise, why have two tables or queries.)

This may seem obvious, but in order to link your two tables or queries, there has to be something that you can link on. Some bit of information that they both share. This is why I have that Master Title table in my database. It creates a link between two vendor tables that wouldn't exist otherwise. If they record my titles differently and use different identifiers then there's no way to directly link those two. But if I create another table that says, X in Table 1 is the same as Y in Table 2, then I can use queries to bring the information from both tables together.

(And, actually, when I rebuilt my database sometime last year I added two sub-Master tables, one for paperbacks and audio and one for ebooks, so that I could handle vendors who provide reports on both print and ebook in the same report. I just make mention of that for any authors out there who might be trying to build their own tracking database. Also, as a reminder that sometimes you have to build in layers in Access to ultimately get to where you want to go.)

Alright. Back to our two tables from above. We need to link these tables. In this case, we're going to link Title to Title.

First, we select the field name from the first table, left-click on it, and drag over to the second table. Ideally you drag over to the field name you want to link on, but in the Relationship workspace you don't have to. Just drag to some field on the second table.

This will bring up the Edit Relationships dialogue box.

On the left-hand side will be the table you started with and the field you started with. On the right-hand side will be the table you dragged to and the field you ended up selecting. In the image above, I accidentally selected Publisher's ISBN instead of Title, but that can easily be fixed by clicking on that field name, pulling up the dropdown menu that's available when I do so, and changing the field selection to the one I want.

(Just a note here that you can also create these relationships or modify them in your query Design View, but the dropdown menu never seems to work for me there.)

Next, we want to specify the join type. Click on Join Type on the right-hand side and tell Access what kind of join this is. You have three options.

We can specify that only information is included when both tables have entries for that join field. (One that I rarely use.) Or we can specify that Access should always include entries from one table or the other and then pull in data from the second table as it matches. What we choose to do will depend on what we want to see.

For example, here is an example where I'm trying to determine what type of relationship to establish between one of my master tables and a vendor table:

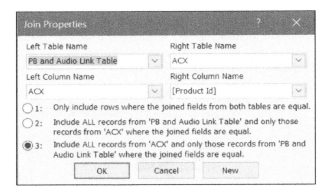

If I include all records from my PB and Audio Link Table and then pull in matching results from the ACX table (which is for audio sales) I'll have blank entries for units and sales for every title that isn't sold in audio or where I haven't had sales yet for that title on ACX.

If I include all records from the ACX table, then I'll only see results for those titles that have had a sale at that vendor.

(We'll explore this further in a minute when we build a query that uses these two tables.)

So choose your Join Type. Then choose OK, and then click Create on the main dialogue box.

(I tend not to click the box to enforce referential integrity because the way I work in my database means I won't always have referential integrity. What enforcing referential integrity does is makes sure that you never have orphaned data. So, for example, if you're using Customer ID, that you never have an entry in your transactions data table with a Customer ID that's not in your customer data table. But because I sometimes have situations where I published a new title and don't yet know what ID a given vendor is going to assign to that title until after it sells, I encounter situations where my report would "break" if I enforced referential integrity. I catch these situations with a set of checks and balances that compare the sum of my sales from each vendor report to my total sales report. If I've just uploaded a new vendor report and my total sales report is $5.32 less than the sum of the individual sales reports then I know I have a book or books that earned me $5.32 during the month where I haven't yet recorded that vendor ID in my master title table for that format.)

Okay. So once you've established a relationship between your two tables or queries, you should see that they are joined by a line.

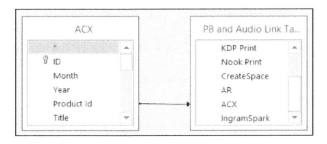

You can double-click on that line at any time to bring up the Edit Relationships box. You can also click on that line and use the Delete key to delete the relationship, although I'd be careful about doing so because it may impact queries you've created that are based on that relationship.

Once you have all of your relationships built, click on Close under the Design tab, and save.

You are now ready to build a query that links data across those two tables or queries.

QUERIES:
QUERIES USING MORE THAN ONE TABLE OR QUERY

First, if you try to create a query using the Query Wizard and more than one table or query and you haven't established a relationship between the two tables or queries, you will get an error message halfway through the process. If that happens, click OK, go create the relationship (as discussed in the prior chapter) and come back to the wizard after you've done so.

Second, know that sometimes you have to build up to the query you want to create. You can't always build the query you want right away.

For example, I have a report that shows total sales by type (print, ebook, audio, and video) for all of my titles. It lists each title, author name, series name, genre, and then units and amount earned by type as well as total units and total amount earned. When I look at that table in Design View I find that it was created using my Title Master table and one query each for my ebook sales, print sales, audio, and video sales. Looking at just the ebook sales query shows that it was created from a report of ebook sales by month which itself was created from twelve separate queries, one for each ebook sales source.

It's possible that someone who was really good at Access or computer programming might be able to build that report with fewer steps, but it's pretty common to find help advice on Access when a query isn't working that says you need to use an intermediate query before building the one you're trying to build.

And what I've found for myself in Access is that I often need to walk my way to the report I want step-by-step by building various queries that roll my data up to higher and higher levels before I can combine the results effectively.

All this said, it means the first query I build for all of my vendors is a sales by month report since most of my vendor data is daily or has multiple entries per product per month. What I want is a report that gives me one line per title and shows me how many copies that title sold on that vendor for that month and how much I earned on them.

Let's go build one of these so you can see how to create a simple summary query using more than one table.

First, go to the Create tab and choose the Query Wizard from the Queries section.

This is still a simple query, so choose the Simple Query Wizard.

Next, select the first table or query that has fields you want to include in your query. In this example that's going to be the Vendor 3 Data Table and I want MonthSale and YearSale.

Switch the dropdown to the other table or query you want to use. In my case that'll be the Ebook Link Table. Select the fields you want from that table. I'm going to choose Title.

Continue to do this until you have all of the fields you want selected. In my case I needed to switch back to the first table and choose Units and Publisher Proceeds.

This is what I end up with:

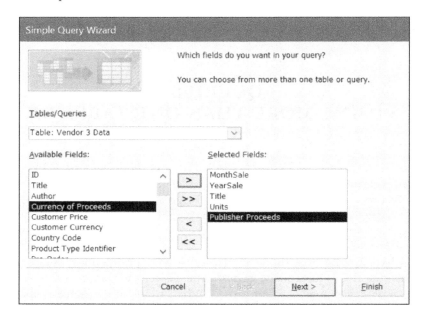

I moved back and forth between the two source tables so that my columns/fields would be in the order I wanted them to be. I could've just as easily added all the ones I wanted from the first table and then all the ones I wanted from the second table and fixed it later in Design View, but I find doing it this way easier.

I should also note here that I didn't have to include the field that linked the two in my selected fields. Just because it's the field being used to link the two tables together doesn't mean it has to be part of the query.

Click Next.

Now, if all you wanted was to pull in the records from the two tables without summarizing anything, you could leave this selected as Detail. But I want this to be a summary query where units sold and amount earned are grouped by title for every month of every year. So I choose Summary and then click on Summary Options.

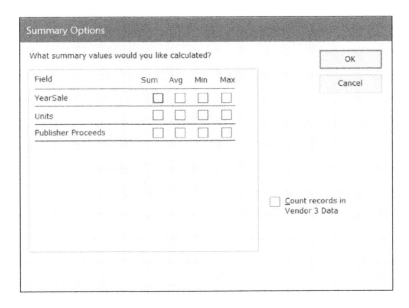

This is what I see. It's important to realize that you may not want to summarize every field that Access suggests to you in the Summary Options screen.

In this case it sees that YearSale is a number so it lists it here. But it doesn't make sense to summarize it, so I just don't check a box for that one.

But I do want the sum for Units and Publisher Proceeds, so I check the sum box for both of them and then click OK.

After that I click Next, I leave the query name alone but you could change it if you want, and then I click Finish.

The query should then open in Datasheet View.

If Access tells you it has to open a query you just created in Design View that's a sign that you have an issue somewhere in your query.

For example, I didn't want to work in my main Access database when I was walking through this example so I uploaded versions of each of these files into a different test database to work with. But that meant that when I completed the wizard it told me I had a type mismatch.

That was because in the Ebook Link Table I had the field type for the vendor identifier as Short Text, but in the vendor data table the vendor identifier was assigned a field type of Number.

After Access told me it had to open in Design View I looked at both tables individually in Design View and compared the field type for the field I was using to link the two tables.

To fix this issue, I had to delete the existing relationship between the tables, change the data type for the vendor identifier field so the two tables matched, save that change to the table design, and then re-create the relationship between the two tables.

After I'd done that I was able to switch my new query to Datasheet view without any issues.

But then I had another concern. At first glance, my table looked like it wasn't pulling in any of the vendor data.

Vendor 3 Data Query1				
MonthSale ▾	YearSale ▾	Title ▾	Sum Of Units ▾	Sum Of Publi: ▾
		Title1		
		Title10		
		Title100		
		Title101		
		Title102		
		Title103		

I had the titles from my master table, but no sales data from the vendor table.

This was because of the relationship join type I had set for the two tables.

I told Access to include all records from my Ebook Link Table and only those records from my vendor table where the join fields were equal. Because the vendor table just had a small number of entries there weren't results for all of the books listed in the Ebook Link Table and the default sort for the query put those results that did exist at the very bottom of the query.

To fix this issue and change the query so that it only showed rows where there were actual results, I went back into Design View for the query, double-clicked on the line between the two tables to bring up the Join Properties dialogue box, and changed the join type to include all records from the vendor table and only those from the Ebook Link Table that matched. When I then went back to Datasheet View, this is what I had:

Vendor 3 Data Query1				
MonthSale ▾	YearSale ▾	Title ▾	Sum Of Units ▾	Sum Of Publi: ▾
November	2019	Title135	1	$10.50
November	2019	Title144	2	$2.80
November	2019	Title154	3	$2.80
November	2019	Title157	3	$2.80
November	2019	Title161	3	$0.70
November	2019	Title2	1	$2.80
November	2019	Title30	1	$3.52
November	2019	Title45	1	$4.16

Every visible row now showed sales data. (Keep in mind, though, that depending on what I was trying to do, that first join type may have been the more appropriate choice. When I create the report of all sales for all vendors for all time, I want it to list all titles even if there does happen to be a title with no sales to report.)

So, bottom line. When you create a query, if something isn't looking the way you want it to, check the join type you're using to see if that fixes things. And if when you go into Datasheet View there is an error or a dialogue box appears asking you to provide a number or Access simply won't do it, then know that something needs to be fixed with respect to your query.

Another quick note here, when you look at a query in Design View you should have the section at the top that shows your tables and their relationships. If you ever open a query in Design View and don't see that section at the top, it's just because the field selection area is taking up the whole space. It's not because it's not there.

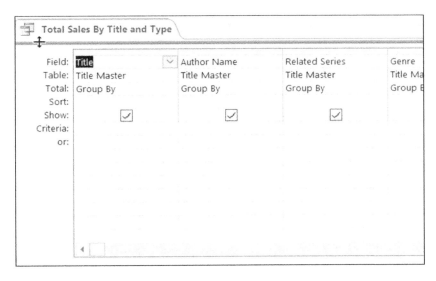

To fix this, hold your cursor over the gray bar right under the tab with the query name until it looks like a bar with arrows pointing upward and downward (as you can see in the screenshot above), left-click, and drag downward until you can see your tables.

If you have to make this change it will be considered a change to the design of the query, so you'll want to save when you exit or you'll have to do it again next time you open the query.

Alright.

* * *

A few more thoughts on building queries that involve more than one table or query.

I prefer to have what I think of as an "anchor" table or query. This is a table or query that all of the other tables and queries I'm going to use can tie to. Like so:

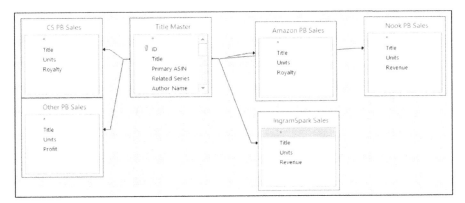

In this example all of the relationships used in this query are between the Title Master table and the five other data sources that are being used to build the query. Note that there are no relationships drawn amongst the other five data sources. I don't have Data Source A linked to Data Source B linked to Data Source C. Everything links directly to Data Source A

I think that having all of my data sources tie back to that one "anchor" table or query eliminates certain issues you can run into with Access around ambiguous joins or double-counting of results.

Even doing it this way, though, I will sometimes run into an issue with my queries where I tell Access to sum the values but access ends up doing so multiple times. So rather than getting an answer of, say 100, I get an answer of 300.

This seems to happen when I'm using a query derived from a query derived from a query. I don't think I've ever had it happen with a query that was derived directly from a data table. I want to say it also only happens when multiple data sources are involved.

I've always been able to fix the issue by having my query display the maximum value in the field rather than the sum, so I've never stopped to nail down exactly what causes that to happen.

But the fact that this can happen is a good reminder to always check your results.

Do not trust blindly that your result in your table is correct just because you think you built it correctly. Have a way to confirm that fact.

The easiest way for me to do this, especially with a summary query, is to compare the result from my source table to my query. If I had a source table that was all sales for vendor X and my query is supposed to be those same sales summarized by title by month, then the total units and total dollar value between the two tables should match.

To easily do this comparison, you need to know how to make Access provide summary values in your tables and queries. Or how to sort and filter. So let's cover that now.

SUMMARY RESULTS, SORTING, AND FILTERING IN A TABLE OR QUERY

When you're working in tables and queries it is often convenient to see the total values of various fields/columns as well as to be able to sort your data or to filter it down to just a subset of the results. I do this all the time for quick checks of my data and also when creating queries to make sure that the results match between my source data and my query.

Summary Results

Let's start with a very basic but powerful option, summarizing the results of a field/column. I use this most often to sum the values in specific fields like units sold.

Summing the values only works if the field is a Number type of field. It will not work on numbers that are stored as text. (And if you're trying to calculate a summary from a query that is pulling information from other queries or tables, those values need to have been designated as a number at every step along the way for this to work. You can't fix it with formatting in the last step.)

To calculate the sum of the values in a field in a table or query, go to the Records section of the Home tab. There is a Totals option there that has the summation mathematical sign next to it. Click on it. This will add a row at the very bottom of your table or query that is labeled Total on the left-hand side.

Scroll over to the column that has the value you want to summarize, click into the cell in that Total row for that column. You'll see a dropdown arrow. Click on it, and you'll see the available options for that column/field.

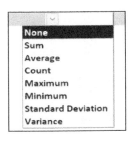

If the field is actually stored as a number, you'll see Sum as one of the available options. Choose it. You will now see the summed value of all entries for that column/field in that cell.

Note from the screenshot above that you also have a choice of Average, Count, Maximum, Minimum, Standard Deviation, and Variance as well as None if you need to remove a summary result that you already added.

If a field is a text field, the only option you're given is Count. For a date field you have Average, Count, Maximum, and Minimum.

I would caution against using any option in that list other than Sum, because there's no way to see that that's what you've done. That row will continue to be labeled Total no matter what choice you make. So you can be taking the average of the values in that column and it will look like you're taking the sum of the values.

To keep the summary row available every time you open that table or query you will need to save changes to the design when you close the table or query.

Sorting

When you tell Access to sort your data you are telling it to display your results in a specific order. For example, I often use the Sort function to display my records alphabetically by title or to display them in descending numeric order so that the most profitable titles are listed first.

You can build a sort into a table or query so that the data is already sorted the way you prefer it to be, but inevitably I find myself wanting to sort my data in some other order at some point.

The type of sort available to you is going to depend on the nature of the data in the column you choose to sort by.

Sort A to Z or Sort Z to A is for "text" entries. That means to sort, as it says, alphabetically from A to Z or reverse alphabetically from Z to A. With an A to Z sort, a row with a value of Apples will display before a row with a value of Oranges in the specified column. With a Z to A sort, the row with Oranges would display before the row with Apples.

Sort Oldest to Newest or Sort Newest to Oldest is for date entries. Again, it's just what it says. If you sort Newest to Oldest the record with the most recent date will display first. If you sort Oldest to Newest the record with the oldest date will display first.

Sort Smallest to Largest or Sort Largest to Smallest is for numeric values. And, again, it's pretty straight-forward. If you Sort Smallest to Largest the smallest value will be first. If you sort Largest to Smallest the largest value will be first.

The nice thing about sorting in Access compared to sorting in Excel is that you don't have to worry about selecting the correct range of data before you sort. All entries in a specific row/record stay together no matter what so you never run the risk of "breaking" your data with a bad sort.

To sort your data, right-click on the column/field you want to use for your sort, and then choose your sort option from the dropdown menu.

If there's already a sort on that column, the chosen type of sort will be highlighted on the left-hand side like so:

See the box around Z to A in that image? That's because the data in question is already sorted on this column using a Z to A sort.

Another option for sorting your columns is to select the column you want to sort by and then choose Ascending or Descending from the Sort & Filter section of the Home tab.

The Sort & Filter section of the Home tab is also where you can go to remove a sort that you have in place. So if you've sorted your data and now want to return it to its original order, you can go to the Sort & Filter section of the Home tab and click on Remove Sort.

There is an option for an Advanced Sort in the Sort & Filter section, but we're not going to cover it here because it's a little complicated.

You can, however, easily sort on more than one column at a time by selecting multiple columns before you choose your sort order. If you do that, all of those columns will sort in the same direction (ascending or descending) according to their nature.

For example, the following data is sorted in an ascending direction on all three columns:

B&N Identifier	DateSale	Title
134567	8/2/2017	Another Title
2345890	8/3/2017	A Third Title
2345890	8/10/2017	A Third Title
123456789	8/1/2017	A Title
123456789	8/1/2017	A Title
123456789	8/2/2017	A Title
123456789	8/3/2017	A Title
123456789	8/6/2017	A Title
123456789	8/6/2017	Check
123456789	8/10/2017	A Title
123456789	8/10/2017	A Title
123456789	8/10/2017	Check

You can see that the data is sorted first by B&N Identifier, then by DateSale, and finally by Title. It's not a perfect method for sorting multiple columns since they need to be side-by-side and the sort has to go in the same direction for all of the selected columns, but it's certainly easier to do than the Advanced Sort option.

Filtering

Filtering is one I use a lot. And if you're familiar with filtering from Excel then you'll pick it right up because it basically works the same way in Access.

Filtering lets you take your table of data and narrow the results down so that only specific results show. I'll often filter for a specific month and year or for a specific title or a specific series name.

To filter your table, click on the small arrow at the end of the column name. This will bring up the dropdown menu for that column which will include the filter options.

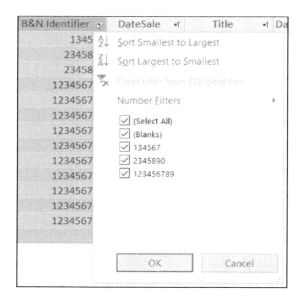

If what you want is a specific value, then click on the box next to Select All. This will unselect all values. And then click on the box next to the value you do want and then click on OK. That should narrow down the data displayed in your table to just the rows/records that match the box you checked.

You can check multiple boxes when you do this. So I'll often use the checkboxes to quickly see the results for a set of titles that are all related.

Sometimes, though, you'll want to filter based on a set of criteria instead. I, for example, often have to filter based on the presence of the text "overdrive" in my title listing for one of my vendors to see what library sales I had.

To do that, depending on the type of data you're dealing with, you'll click on the small arrow at the end of the column name to bring up the dropdown menu and then place your cursor over either Date Filters, Number Filters, or Text Filters as the case may be.

This will display a secondary dropdown menu off to the side of the original dropdown menu.

Here's the one for Text Filters:

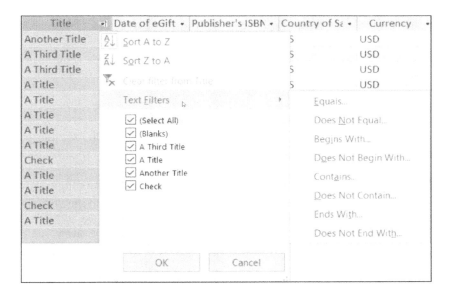

From there, choose the filter type you want. When I'm looking for titles that have "overdrive" in them I choose the Contains option because that will look for the word overdrive anywhere in the text of each entry.

Equals has to be an exact match. Does Not Equal has to not be an exact match. Begins With has to start with that value. Does Not Begin With must not start with that value. Does Not Contain doesn't contain that value anywhere. Ends With must end with that value. And Does Not End With must not end with the value.

The filters for Dates and Numbers are slightly different but work on the same principles.

Whichever one you choose, Access will then display a Custom Filter dialogue box where you type the criteria it needs to use. For text the value is not case-sensitive so Overdrive and overdrive are treated the same.

Another way to access the Filter dropdown menu is by clicking on Filter in the Sort & Filter section of the Home tab. It's only an available option if you're clicked into a single cell of your data table or have selected a single column. Clicking on the Filter option will open the dropdown menu in the table for that column just like right-clicking does.

To remove a filter you already applied, you can click on the filter symbol on the right-hand side of the column name to bring up the filter dropdown menu and then choose "Clear Filter from [Field]" where [Field] is the column name. That will remove the filter for that one column.

To temporarily remove all filters from your table or query, you can click on the Filtered option at the bottom of the data table.

(This is also an easy place to check to see if your table is currently filtered. If it says Filtered, it is. If it says Unfiltered or No Filter, it isn't.)

Clicking on that option only temporarily removes the filter. You can click on Unfiltered in the exact same spot to put the filter(s) back.

To permanently remove all filters from the table go to the Sort & Filter section of the Home tab, click on the arrow under Advanced, and choose Clear All Filters from the dropdown menu.

* * *

One final note about sorting or filtering in Access. When you sort or filter a table or query, even if you then return the table or query to its original appearance, when you go to close that table or query Access will ask, "Do you want to save changes to the design of [X]?"

Note that this is not asking you about saving changes to your data. The minute you change a data entry in a table or query, that change has been saved. This is just about changing the sort order or keeping a filter on your data or keeping a new column order. Usually my answer on this is "No" unless I was deliberately working to change the appearance of that table or query.

QUERIES:
USING SIMPLE CRITERIA TO NARROW DOWN RESULTS

There are going to be times when you want to build a query that doesn't just summarize the results from other tables or queries, but actually only displays a subset of those results.

For example, I don't want to include in my units sold numbers any books that I've given away for free. Because I don't consider those sales. So in all of my queries that pull from my vendor reports I exclude any books that were priced at free. (I have separate reports for those.)

To do this, I use the Criteria row in the Design View for the query in question. I build my query like I normally would using the Query Wizard and then make my edits in Design View when I have a query to work with.

In Access there is a help topic called *Examples of Query Criteria* that I would urge you to review if you're going to use criteria, but let me cover some of the basics here.

Here is an example of a query that uses criteria in the first column and in the last column:

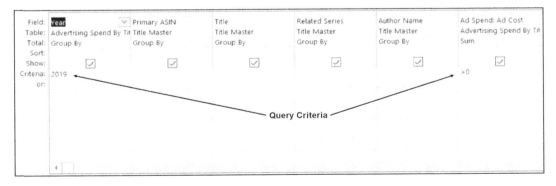

The first column, Year, specifies that I only want to pull in values where the year has a value of 2019.

The last column, which is advertising cost, specifies that I only want to pull in values that are greater than zero.

Both of these are examples of numeric criteria. For numbers, listing just the number looks for an exact match. You can also use the greater than and less than operators > and < or >= and <= to specify only values greater than a certain amount or less than a certain amount. Including the equals sign makes that greater than or equal to or less than or equal to.

For multiple criteria you can use AND or OR which mean that the value must meet both listed criteria (for AND) or one of the list of choices (for OR).

You can also use NOT followed by a number value to exclude a specific numeric result.

When dealing with text, you need to use quotes around the text. So, for example,

"Excel"

will return all records where the entry in that field exactly matches the text in the quotes, Excel.

Any additional text in the cell would prevent a match. So, if my actual value was Excel for Beginners, Access would not include the entry. To have Access return a result that contains the word Excel anywhere in the field, I'd have to add wildcards to the text in quotes. In this case

"*Excel*"

would return any field that contains the word Excel anywhere within the text.

Note the use of the * at both the beginning and the end is the wildcard. That is telling Access any number of characters before and any number of characters after the specified word.

A ? wildcard just stands for one character. You can use multiple ? wildcards together if needed. So,

"???Excel*"

would return any record where there were up to three characters, including spaces before the word and then any number of characters after it. So, *An Excel Adventure* would be a match. *Excel Adventures* would not.

Access has a tendency to modify the criteria you enter to match its display preferences. So if you enter "*Excel*" as your criteria, when you go back into Design View you will see that Access has taken your entry and added the word Like at the beginning of it to make:

Like "*Excel*"

There is another option, Not Like, that lets you exclude results. So typing in

Not Like "*Excel*"

would exclude any result that had Excel anywhere in the field.

For more than one entry you can separate them with OR. So typing in

"*Excel*" OR "*Access*"

would pull all entries with either Excel or Access anywhere in them.

AND can serve the same purpose except then all of the listed criteria must be there for the entry to be included. Using

"*Excel*" AND "*Access*"

would mean the entry has to have both words, Excel and Access, to be shown.

In general, when I need to use a criteria for a specific purpose I go and look up exactly how to do it rather than try to remember all the different criteria that can be used and how they're written. That help topic in Access is a very good place to start. There are also some great online resources I've found when needed over the years.

PRINTING, FORMS, AND REPORTS:
A BRIEF DISCUSSION

There are going to be times when you want to do more than just look at your data in your Access database and instead want to print a physical copy of the data or maybe even send a PDF file to someone else.

If you think you will routinely want to do this with the same set of information, then a report is your best bet. A report can be generated from a table, a query, or a form.

To create a basic Report, click on the table, query, or form that you're going to use, go to the Create tab, and click on Report in the Reports section. This will give you a very basic report that has all of the fields from source table, query, or form. (You can also use the Report Wizard if you want more control over which fields are included or if you want to include grouping, sorting, or summation values or have more control over layout at the report creation stage.)

It's beyond the scope of this book to cover how to then delete fields, format fields, etc. but that can definitely be done and will be covered in detail in *Intermediate Access*. For now, know that the simple steps I outlined above will turn your source data into a basic report and that you can then work in Design View for that report to turn it into something more customized.

The main issue with working with a report generated with the Report option is that it generally won't print neatly onto a single page. You're very likely to have columns of data that continue on to a second or even a third page.

Another option, and one that I used early on when I was more comfortable in Excel than I was in Access, is to export your table or query to Excel and create a printed and formatted document from there. I personally think that Excel is far more friendly when it comes to printing raw data than Access is.

One of the reasons I found this approach most useful was because at the printing stage Excel has the scaling option that lets me force my data onto a specified number of pages in width or height. Access does not. In Access the number of pages that your data takes up when it prints is determined by your column widths and the font size of your text. There is no proportional scaling when you go to print to make it fit.

Because of that little difference it takes far more time and effort to create a good-looking report in Access than it does in Excel.

So for me, how often I'll need the report and how heavily customized it needs to be drives whether I simply export to Excel or take the time to create a report in Access.

* * *

To print from Access, open the table, query, form, or report that you want to print, go to File, and choose Print. This will give you the option to Quick Print, Print, or Print Preview. ALWAYS use print preview in Access. You will save yourself a lot of wasted paper by doing so.

Here is a simple print preview of a query:

At the bottom of the main workspace you can see where it says Page and then there are arrows. This lets you page through your printed document to see what each printed page will look like when there is more than one page. In this case, when I move to the second page I found one column of data on its own page.

In this case it was easily fixed by changing the Page Layout to Landscape in the Page Layout section of the Print Preview tab.

(That's always something I check for in Access because it happens often.)

If that doesn't work, changing the Margins to Narrow in the Page Size section can sometimes force all of the columns of data onto a single page. To do this, click on the arrow under Margins and choose Narrow.

Other than that, though, you're somewhat limited on your printing options in Access compared to Excel which is why if you're going to do a lot of printing from Access it's best to create a report.

If you can get the document looking good enough to print from your print preview, then click on Print in the top left corner to bring up the Print dialogue box. This is where you can specify which pages to print if you don't want them all, the number of copies to print, and, under Properties, that you want to print on both sides of the page.

I often move in and out of the Print Preview when I'm designing a Report because making sure all my columns will fit on a single page is usually the biggest challenge.

Okay.

* * *

The one other item we haven't covered yet and are not going to cover in detail but need to touch on is forms. Forms are good for when you want to separate your records into single pages that can be printed one at a time or for when you have a lot of text-based information that you're going to be entering directly in Access or needing to review regularly.

To create a basic form, go to a table or query, click on it, then choose Form from the Forms section of the Create tab. This will create for you a basic form with one page per record.

If you used a data table or a basic detail query to create the form, you can edit the values directly in the form and your changes will carry through to the underlying data table.

If it was a summary query you used to generate the form, you can see the data in the form, but won't be able to edit it.

If you want multiple records to show on a single form page, you can use the More Forms dropdown menu in the Forms section of the Create tab and choose Multiple Items from the dropdown. This will put your records in rows instead of separated onto different pages.

To navigate between pages in a form, use the arrows at the bottom of the workspace. You can further edit your forms in Design View. (This is covered in detail in *Intermediate Access*.)

WHERE TO GET ADDITIONAL INFORMATION

This book was just a beginner guide to Access. It was not by any means meant to be a comprehensive guide. The goal here was to make you comfortable with moving around in Access and to give you the ability to work with tables and basic queries.

But Access can do a whole lot more than that.

So where do you go from here?

If you want to continue working with me then your next step should be *Intermediate Access* which will cover topics like union queries, crosstab queries, and append queries as well as how to customize forms and reports.

But if you just have a specific question you need answered there are a number of other options available to you.

One is the built-in help that's right there in Access.

Often if you hold your mouse over an item, Access will give you a brief description of what it does. Sometimes those descriptions come with a Tell Me More option. Like this one for Tables in the Create tab:

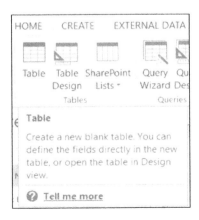

If you click on that Tell Me More text, it will open for you an Access Help pane covering that specific topic. In this case it opens to a help topic titled *Create a Table and Add Fields*.

Your other option within Access is to go straight to the Access Help screen. You can do this by clicking on the question mark in the top right corner. This will open Access Help and give you both a search box as well as top categories of information.

F1 (if you have your F keys available by default which is not always the case in newer computers) will also open Access Help.

If that's not enough, because sometimes it isn't a question of how something works but can something be done, you can always search online. I recommend including your Access version in your search and seeing if Microsoft support has a solution before you branch out from there.

So search for something like "add fixed value query Access 2013 microsoft support" and then choose the support.microsoft.com or support.office.com result that matches your search.

But while Microsoft is very good at discussing how things work, they often fail to address what is possible.

But there are plenty of free forums and websites out there that do cover those kinds of questions, and chances are your question has probably already been asked before.

Just keep in mind that the internet is full of jerks who sometimes can act very condescending and rude when answering questions so it's always better to find someone else who already asked your question than subject yourself to that, at least as far as I'm concerned. (This is why I usually will try and fail a dozen times on my own rather than go to one of those user boards to see if someone knows the answer already.)

But, worst case scenario, you can always ask your question on one of the user forums that are out there. If you do so, just be as precise as possible about what you want to know and be sure to mention the version of Access you're working with and be as clear on your terminology as you can be.

You can also try me. I may already know the answer or be able to find it for you fairly easily. Just know that I won't open someone else's Access database so it needs to be a question I can answer without needing access to your database.

CONCLUSION

Alright. So that's it. That's how to approach the basics of Microsoft Access if you're someone like me who is used to working in Excel but needs an option that lets them combine data in more complicated ways than Excel allows for.

This book is much longer than the equivalent books I've written for Excel, Word, and PowerPoint simply because Access is much more complex to work with and requires a lot more beginner-level knowledge to work in it effectively.

Just a few reminders.

Keep your original data safe somewhere else so that you always have it to go back to.

If that isn't possible, be sure to regularly save back-ups of your database.

Work with caution in Access because so many changes that you make in Access are permanent and cannot be undone.

Expect to make mistakes. I personally find Access more finicky than Excel which means that on a somewhat regular basis I have to deal with different error messages and troubleshoot them. It's okay if that happens. Google is your friend if you need to understand what a message is telling you or why something didn't look the way it should.

Also, be sure that you have checks and balances in your database or elsewhere that let you confirm that your queries are working. It's somewhat easy with Access to drop data and not know that you have if you aren't doing these types of checks.

So check and verify and proceed with caution.

But have confidence that you can work through it and make it work. And remember that Access, while intimidating to a new user, is an incredibly powerful tool that is worth mastering.

Good luck!

INDEX
(In addition to the categories listed in the Table of Contents)

ABOUT THE AUTHOR

M.L. Humphrey is a former stockbroker with a degree in Economics from Stanford and an MBA from Wharton who has spent close to twenty years as a regulator and consultant in the financial services industry.

You can reach M.L. at mlhumphreywriter@gmail.com or at mlhumphrey.com.